"Being Loved Shouldn't Hurt"

Recognize and Overcome Toxic Relationships So You Can Live Your Best Life Now

by

Stephanie McPhail, M.S.

Printed in the United States of America

First Printing May 2018

ISBN-10:1987770048

CreateSpace for Amazon

www.mindandbodyawakenings.com

FOREWORD by: *Tamara Montana*, Marriage and Family Therapist; Heart Virtue Expert; Interior Designer and Facilitator with husband Greg Montana in Workshops/Seminars/Marriage Retreats/Cruises and author of: *Emerald Echo, Beyond this World there is a World I want...*

Congratulations for picking up this book! Imagine...the title of Stephanie's book is actually true. Being genuinely loved doesn't ever have to hurt. I have great respect for the journey you are about to encounter through Stephanie's experiences of tragedy to triumph. My husband Greg and I share on many platforms that "Your Pain, is Your Credential." If you've **healed** from a specific pain, you've earned the right to help others through similar tunnels of darkness. Domestic Violence and Emotional Abuse can leave devastating wounds that may require additional help to overcome. If there are any questions about whether you are in an abusive relationship or not, this book will be a lighthouse in the middle of a storm.

As a licensed psychotherapist, many years ago I learned: As water seeks its own level, so does self-esteem in relationships. We are unconsciously attracted to what is familiar. We tell others how to treat us, by the way, we treat ourselves.

This next statement I'm about to make may seem odd at first glance, but consider... What if: All my experiences are happening **for** me, and not to me? This one idea can open a space for taking responsibility in order to choose again. *The Course in Miracles* says: We don't ever have to seek for love outside of ourselves, *love is who we are...* we just have to remove the blocks that prevent us from seeing the love we are... You were created in love, born in love and will eventually return to love. When this truth vibrates in every cell of our being, we will not tolerate abusive treatment in ourselves or another.

Abusive treatment matches the erroneous belief, the lie we adopt that says: "I don't matter." But when we're able to re-discover our non-negotiable God given worth, that is not dependent on anyone or anything outside of ourselves, the label inside can be revealed: "Made in Love."

Our worth that gets covered up and buried inside, happens when we hold grievances towards ourselves or another. When we emotionally put another in jail, neither the jailer nor the prisoner is free. One recent definition I heard of forgiveness: Giving up all hope of a different past. Forgiving those who have hurt us, opens a door for us to forgive ourselves... Forgive ourselves for taking disrespectful treatment we don't deserve.

As we evolve and ultimately realize there is no one to blame, we are free. Free to attract relationships that treat us with genuine love, respect and beautiful boundaries. When we realize whatever has happened is no one's fault, **_but it is our responsibility_**, we will stand for beautiful relationships that honor our purpose and encourage each other to show up as their highest version.

Stephanie's story will lead you to what's possible in relationships when we discover our God given worth.

Preface

For a long time, I hid my past out of fear and embarrassment. I didn't want anyone to know that I was vulnerable. I had always kept up the ability to take care of myself, or so it would seem from an outsider. Little did anyone know that I was living in my own personal hell. I was able to go out and do good for so many people but I was not able to create a romantic relationship where I felt safe and at ease. I was struggling, trying to live the best way I could while feeling my home wasn't my safe place. A lot of people could tell something wasn't right but I would never give anyone all of the details; saying it out loud made it more real to me. It's isolating when you feel too ashamed to talk about things that are really hurting you.

It took a long time for me to open up about everything I went through. I had a lot of healing to do before I could be comfortable dealing with the consequences of speaking up. Once I started to share my story with others, it opened up the possibility for them to share theirs. I realized how many people are in a very similar situation. I wrote this book to give hope. Sometimes it feels like what we dream is impossible; we feel trapped in the situation, feeling like there's no way out. I found that things can change if we start to take an active role in our own happiness.

My passion in life is to help other women move past unhealthy relationships and live their best life. I have a Double Master's Degree in Health and Education, a Bachelor's degree in Psychology, I'm a Certified Crisis Counselor and a Transformational Coach. My personal experiences with toxic relationships, as well as my schooling and training, allows me to empathize with others while helping them heal and move on.

It can be scary to make big changes, but to me, not living your best life is even scarier. Everything that happens in our lives can either be used to help us grow or keep us trapped; the choice is ours. I chose to learn the lessons and am now living a life I barely thought was possible. I found that letting go of blame and anger towards myself and others was integral to the journey.

Acknowledgments

I would like to thank my amazing husband David for his unwavering support in everything I do! It's such a wonderful experience having a partner who helps motivate me to be the best version of myself. I'm reminded daily how lucky I am to have found you and share this journey with you. I'm eternally grateful to see that the dream is real.

Thank you to my son Zachary and new baby for giving me the privilege of being your mom and helper on your own journeys.

Thank you to my family; I always hope that I make you proud even when we may not always agree.

Thank you to my best friends Brooke and Sharon and all the other friends who have supported me throughout the years. You are amazing for a long list of reasons. I am thoroughly thankful for your friendship; you are my chosen family.

Thank you for all of the life lessons that have brought me to the place I am at now.

Introduction

I never heard the word "codependent" until my first husband told me that's what I was. I remember being insulted without really knowing exactly what it meant. Oddly enough, once I did the research, I realized he was right. It was the only reason I had stayed in a toxic relationship as long as I did. As the CEO of Mind and Body Awakenings, a holistic healing and coaching business, I talk intimately with people daily about their lives. In speaking to these clients, friends, listening to music, and watching popular movies, I have come to realize this mindset is all too common. Many people stay in their codependent relationships or leave only to repeat it in their next relationship. I'd like to share my story from my perspective along with the story of three other people who got out, broke the pattern, and are currently living happy lives!

My intention for this book is to share experiences and share information so that you can recognize and overcome toxic relationships, so you can live your best life now! Take notes while you are reading and stop anytime you need to journal when something comes up for you. The life you dream of is not only possible but waiting for you if you take the right steps. By the time you are done reading this book, you will have a whole new view on how to take the right action steps in creating your best new life and living your life purpose!

Being Loved Shouldn't Hurt is meant to be a quick read to educate the reader on unhealthy relationships, explain how to get out of the cycle, and help to find your true self again. This book also shows that being in love shouldn't equate to pain and disappointment. Learning how to love yourself will help you not return to those destructive relationships. Living your happily ever after is possible!

Table of Contents

"Being Loved Shouldn't Hurt"

PART ONE

Chapter 1
My Story

I didn't have a very good example of what a healthy relationship looked like growing up. My parents fought regularly. Overall, they seemed to simply "tolerate" each other more than share a deep friendship and love for one another. Despite that, my parents are still together. They love each other the best way they know how. I'm sure, like most of us, they learned how to love from their parents who learned from their parents and so on. In fact, stories going back on both sides of the family were filled with abuse and unhealthy situations. I hoped to break the cycle and go down a different path. The problem is, when you're trained from a young age to behave a certain way, it's hard to change. It requires a conscious effort to do things differently. It's common for people in unhealthy relationships to come from a long lineage of the same patterns. We do what we know. I had friends growing up whose parents got along really well. This gave me hope that it was possible to have a calm quiet home, but in the back of my mind, I wondered if something flawed in me would keep me from having one.

The first time I remember desperately wanting a boyfriend was in high school. I had trouble "fitting in." All the other girls seemed to have boyfriends, so I wanted one too. This led me to lose my virginity at a young age since I had the preconceived notion that everyone else was having sex as well. Throughout high school, I continued to have sexual relationships instead of committed relationships. My viewpoint on what was normal was skewed.

I was 19 years old when I met my first real boyfriend. My friends and I were at a club; from across the room, I saw a very tall guy with red hair. Big Red had a good energy about him that I liked right away. As an excuse to talk to him, I went over to ask for the time and he stumbled over the answer. It was endearing. He was the first guy that I had spoken to in a long time that looked into my eyes instead of at my boobs. Big Red answered and I stood there awkwardly for a few seconds, waiting to see his next move. He remained silent. I thought, maybe he's just not available. I started to walk away from him when he asked me where I lived. We spent the rest of the evening talking each other's ears off. It was an instant connection. When we talked, it was like time stood still. We would spend hours on the phone; calls were like an escape from the world around us. Within two weeks the "I Love You"s started and we became exclusive right away.

The first few years were more wonderful than I could have imagined. We were best friends and we both liked to have a good time. The big difference was that I knew how to balance fun and work, and he didn't. As time progressed, the issues started to become apparent, but I ignored them.

One of the first red flags I experienced was when we were all hanging out with friends one night. Big Red got jealous and angry that I was talking more to one of my female friends - he thought I was flirting with her. This was almost two years into our relationship and I had never seen this side of him before. We talked it out and things seemed to get better. We kept moving forward.

Another red flag I noticed but did nothing about, was how unhealthy his parents' marriage was. His father was deceitful. His mother took care of and explained away everything he did. His father passed away from lung cancer because he was still secretly smoking even though he had said he quit numerous times. I remember sitting in the hospital room one of the many times he was rushed there and thinking, this could be me in 25 years if I stay in this relationship. For some reason, I still didn't break it off.

One night we went out to a club for my best friend's graduation party. When my boyfriend walked away, a guy came over and wanted to play "pass the lifesaver" with my friend. I knew it would turn into kissing; I was 25 years old, unsure of myself, and anxious about what to do. I didn't want to seem uncool and say no, but I also knew that my boyfriend would not be happy. Before I could think of an excuse, this guy's mouth was on mine "passing a lifesaver." Big Red was watching from the other side of the room. Instead of asking me what happened, he got angry and accused me of cheating on him. I had felt uncomfortable telling the guy to get away from me but looking back, I should have gone with my gut and said no. I didn't know how to stand up for myself. This wouldn't be the first time I didn't follow my gut and then had to deal with the negative consequences because of it. That fight lasted almost two weeks, filled with screaming, crying, and a lot of hurt feelings. I should've broken it off with him then but we were living together and I felt like I had to make it work. I also felt guilty that I had allowed this guy to do that and I didn't do anything. My shame and guilt kept me from making a better decision.

I had gotten money from a car accident I was in when I was 18. I decided that I wanted to invest the money in a house. My dad offered to be a cosigner for me on the loan but even after all of the red flags I had already seen, I asked Big Red to cosign with me. I figured I had the money and he had the ability to fix up a house. Between the two of us, we could flip it and make some money! In my mind, him being a partial owner would inspire him to work harder. It wasn't long before his laziness became a huge fighting point. I kept asking him to start work on what needed to be fixed up on the house; he felt like I was nagging him. Over a year went by and nothing was done.

I was going to college to work on my Master's degree and he was going to his friend's house all the time to smoke pot. He had even started to sell it. Not only did I not want him to get arrested, but I also didn't want anything like that around me! I had a career I was working towards and I didn't want his bad decisions to keep me from my goal. Big Red kept selling behind my back. It seemed to be something he'd learned from his father, and it scared the hell out of me. As much as I didn't want to be like his mom, trying so hard to keep the family together, here I was doing the same thing. For some reason, I still didn't break up with him.

I continued to stay, despite the sneakiness, bad temper, and overall hurtful nature that had become the new "normal". When we moved in together, we agreed I would pay our bills at the house and he would pay me back for half of it. He hadn't paid for two or three months and I was starting to get nervous. He kept saying he didn't have the money. One day, I opened up his bank statement, thinking it was mine (we had the same bank). I stared in disbelief at the thousands of dollars in his account. I confronted him; he said he was saving up to buy an All Terrain Vehicle he wanted. I lost it! How could he do this knowing how worried I was about keeping up with our bills? Still, I let him stay.

"Being Loved Shouldn't Hurt"

Once his father passed away, Big Red became more angry, defensive, and withdrawn. There were several occasions where, in a fit of rage, he pushed me, threatened me, and punched holes in the walls around my head. His favorite words to use when he was angry with me was to call me a whore and a bitch. I tried to explain it away by saying he was having a hard time dealing with the death of his father. But as time continued to move on he was still behaving badly.

Two years after the death of his father, things had only gotten worse. We had really lost connection and didn't spend a lot of time together. I was still desperately trying to hold onto a failing relationship out of loyalty and fear that I couldn't keep up with payments on the house without him. I decided I could no longer sit at home waiting for him to come home. I needed to go out and be social. It was time to go out again, even if it meant going out alone. I went out with some friends and before we went, I spoke on the phone with Big Red. He admitted he wasn't being super reliable. I told him that he could be so wonderful when things were good but that when he withdrew and got defensive, he was horrible to be around. I said to him, "please, don't let my good guy go bad." Big Red seemed to really understand where I was coming from and promised he would come and meet me out with my friends.

Night came and so did the agreed upon time of departure. I waited for an hour and a half and he never showed up. I wasn't going to spend another night alone waiting for him to come home. I went out and had a good time with friends. A few hours into the night, I got a strange message from someone saying that my boyfriend was banging on the door of my friend's house. I kind of ignored it, thinking there must be some kind of explanation - maybe he was still trying to meet up with us?

I got home around 1:30 in the morning. He wasn't home so I changed into my pajamas and went to bed. It had become more normal for him to disappear so I didn't think much of it. About an hour later, he arrived. He turned on the lights, ripped my blankets off, and jerked me out of bed by my shirt so hard the buttons popped off. He yelled at me, called me horrible names, and accused me of cheating. I didn't know where any of this was coming from, especially since I had invited him to come out with us and he was the one who hadn't shown up! Big Red was in a fit of rage, saying he had gone to my friend's apartment and saw me having sex on the couch. I hadn't even gone to that friend's house.

Big Red didn't believe me and wanted to call the people I said I was out with. It was 2:30 in the morning! While he stared angrily at me, I called one of my friends. I told her that he was accusing me of cheating and was losing his mind. He took my phone and threw it across the room; it shattered. My friend got so worried when she couldn't call me back that she called the police.

The police arrived shortly after 3 am. When they got there, they saw Big Red was still very angry and I was still clutching my pajama top closed. They took a report and asked him to leave the house. As one of the officers walked out of the house he said, "You're too young to feel this way; get out while you can." That was enough to make me decide it was over. I was embarrassed my friend had to call the police but also very grateful she had made that decision. It was a wake up call. A few days later, I packed a bunch of my things and moved to a friend's house. It was the only way that I could get away because he refused to leave the house.

I started getting phone calls - sometimes more than 30 times a day. If Big Red found out I was seeing someone, he would call them to say I had a sexually transmitted disease or that I was a whore. His scare tactics made it hard to date. He would follow me. Even when I was traveling, if I saw a car that was similar to his, I'd get anxious immediately. Finally, I got an order of protection. Things started to improve, especially after he argued for half of the house that I had paid for and got $120K. The money didn't matter to me. I just wanted to have no connection to him anymore. I was still getting calls so I changed my number.

Stephanie McPhail

At this point, I was 27 years old. I had been dating my ex boyfriend for over seven years. I didn't know how to date since I'd been with the same person since I was a teenager and was out of the loop for so long! I neglected to take the time to work on myself and heal from that relationship. Instead, I told myself I wasn't interested in having a relationship. I would just casually date and have sex. Great plan right? It may have been better if I actually followed it!

The next guy I dated was a co-worker at the school (I was a teacher at this time). He had the same name as my ex-boyfriend; that should have been my first red flag. The second clue should have been the first night we went out. I got completely blackout drunk (will never know if he actually put something in my drink) and we had sex. I wasn't someone who slept with just anybody, especially not on the first date. I felt really bad the next day when I woke up with him next to me in bed and I didn't remember what happened! What did I do? I forced myself to see where things could go with him even though I wasn't 100% sure. Music Teacher was the kind of guy that people liked. He had great connections, was funny, and was a really good musician -- all qualities I liked in a man. I figured it would be good for me to date someone that I wasn't completely attracted to on the physical level, that maybe I needed to be less superficial? I decided to give it a chance and see where it could go.

"Being Loved Shouldn't Hurt"

Music Teacher wanted to be exclusive right away. He was very pushy about wanting to take me places and meet his family. I was still having a hard time trying to figure out if I even liked the guy. He invited me on an all expense paid trip to Disney. I said no many times, but he kept pushing until I finally said yes. The trip was awful. He made me cry several times, trying to make me feel bad for going on the trip when I wouldn't date him exclusively. The more I would push away, the harder he would try.

He becomes very jealous of any male I spoke to. At one point, I had told him about my ex-boyfriend calling me incessantly and then hanging up. I started to get those phone calls again. I got tired of his drama and broke it off with him.

Music Teacher showed up at my house and threatened to kill himself in my driveway if I didn't date him. I refused, telling him I'd call the police if he showed up again. He would come into my classroom once a day and embarrass me in front of my students, trying to cause a scene. He even went so far as to tell me he had a naked picture of me on his phone! He threatened that if I didn't date him he would put it out on social media so everyone could see. I was overwhelmed; maybe this was just the type of men I attracted! I was afraid to tell my superiors because I was untenured and was afraid to lose my job. I didn't want to cause a scene because of my poor judgment in seeing someone from work.

I finally had enough. If I couldn't change anything about my work life, I would at least stop the 30+ phone calls that were coming in every day. I still had the order of protection against my ex-boyfriend, but they had told me that unless I heard his voice during a call that I couldn't do anything. I was done feeling powerless and finally told the court that I heard Big Red's voice on one of the calls. With that, the order was violated. When I did this, I was so sure it was my long term ex. I didn't even think it could be anyone else. Much to my surprise, I got a phone call from my lawyer telling at work and told him what the court had found. He tried to deny it of course, so I asked to see his phone records. He refused. I went straight to my union representative and told them. I knew I needed more protection because I wasn't sure what else he was capable of doing.

The next day, someone I worked with came to me and said Music Teacher had told her he was going to have his friend, who was a cop, follow me. He also offered to show her the naked picture of me. She wasn't going to allow his madness to continue and was going to go straight to my principal. She reassured me that it was for my own protection if he did anything rash.

I was called in and asked about everything that had been happening. I was also told I was not the only woman at work he was harassing. It was so embarrassing to tell them about his attempt to blackmail me with the picture, but it was a relief to finally have it out in the open. Within a day he was let go from his position. Had I pushed my fear aside and said something right away to my boss, things could have been taken care of earlier without having to deal with harassment. My fear kept me from taking the step.

There I was 27 years old, and two relationships in a row had turned crazy. I felt like I had wasted so much time; I also felt like I was to blame. Why was I attracting such negative people? Why weren't good guys attracted to me? Maybe they didn't exist. Or what if they did exist and I brought out the crazy in men? Maybe it was my fault. You tell yourself a lot of things when you're trying to make sense of a bad situation.

I didn't realize I still had a lot of issues to work out, including guilt from my first major relationship. I fell back into the pattern of having a good time but not really looking within. I started dating again. I saw friends starting to settle down and get married. I was starting to feel like I was getting older and I'd be alone. I was more worried about being alone and neglected when I should have been working on loving myself.

My house was "the place to be." I owned my own home and was always hosting parties, more so now that I was single. There were constantly new people coming over and plenty of guys were showing interest. I was feeling pretty good about myself, I thought.

I became good friends with a guy that came over often. He was super smart, a great dancer, and was also single so we ended up doing a lot of things together. I wished I was attracted to him, but I wasn't. On my birthday, actually my first birthday as a single girl, I invited him to come out. He asked if his newly-single best friend could come and hang out with us. Of course, I agreed right away.

The day before we were going to go out, a different friend showed up at my front door. For the sake of this story, I'll call him "Billy." Billy had been in trouble with the law and didn't always hang around with the right people. He wasn't a "good guy" by society's standards. I had met him while out with friends one night. I thought they knew him so I invited him back to my house for the afterparty. He later told me that he'd gone out that night feeling like he was going to kill himself, but because he met me, he didn't. After that, he'd come over to gossip, hang out, and help clean my house. He was like one of my girlfriends.

One day he called me from jail and said he needed to be picked up because of a DWI. I told him that I would help him, but he only had one "get out of jail free" card from me. After that day, he stopped coming around.

"Being Loved Shouldn't Hurt"

So now here we are, back to the day before my birthday in December. Billy showed up on my doorstep. I invited him to come out for my birthday; he accepted. He said he knew people at the club who would get us in for free and we wouldn't have to pay for drinks. Sounded like a pretty nice deal for my birthday!

The next day everyone showed up and said their pleasant "hellos". Once at the club, we were let in for free and got free drinks. We had a great time celebrating my first single birthday since I was 19. We all went back to my house to relax in the hot tub. We were talking and having a great time, at least I thought so.

Billy suddenly got out of the tub without a word. We assumed he was going to bed. The sun started to come up and it seemed it was time to end the party. We got out of the hot tub, dried off, and went into my living room. We looked in one of the guest bedrooms and didn't see Billy, but didn't think much of it. We sat down on the couch and the friend of a friend said he wanted to go outside and smoke a cigarette. As he was standing outside, we heard him say "Hey, where did we park your car when we came back?" My friend and I looked at each other and said at the same time "Billy stole the car." It was gone and so was Billy.

No one should have been driving a car at any point that night after we got home; we were very concerned for his safety and the safety of others on the road. Since Billy had friends in all the wrong places, we were afraid to call the police for obvious reasons. What to do? We called all the local hospitals looking for someone in a car accident. Nothing. We came to the conclusion that we had no choice but to call the police and file a report. Once we filed the report, I called Billy's mom, hoping he had gone back home. Nothing. The three of us spent the day together repeating the phrase "Billy stole the car" over and over again in disbelief.

Late that night, I got a call from Billy's mom. He was at her house with the car and wanted us to know it was okay. We breathed a collective sigh of relief and left quickly to pick it up nearly 30 minutes away. He returned it with barely any gas left in the tank, but not a scratch on it. After that, I never saw him again.

The three of us had shared an experience that most people couldn't imagine going through. I think that after an ordeal like that, it's a bit easier to feel a connection to people. Therefore, I'd grown a crush on my friend's friend. We spoke to each other a few times on the phone and decided there was chemistry. When I told my friend he said, "Date anyone, just don't date my best friend." I didn't want to lose my friendship with him, but I also didn't want to be kept from someone who may be a great guy for me, I had no idea why he was trying to warn me. I naturally felt comfortable around him purely because he was a good friend's best friend. Plus, he had been around at other parties and always seemed to be fun. However, I should have taken my friend's warning more seriously!

I was the one who made the first move. He acted nervous to be around me so I kept trying to make him feel less insecure. Things moved quickly. It wasn't long before "I love you" was being said and I was being introduced to his mom. Despite this, I had a feeling in my gut that something wasn't right.

The first time I saw a red flag was less than 4 months into our relationship. A bunch of friends wanted to go dancing like we did often. We were having a great time when his friend brought over someone he knew - a tall muscular, good looking guy. It turned out I knew him too. I had met him months ago when I was single. I said hello and introduced him to my boyfriend. The tension was visible in the air and very uncomfortable. It was rather quickly that everyone parted ways. My now-boyfriend (let's call him Richard) was visibly unhappy, so I asked him what was going on. He told me that I'd allowed that guy to disrespect him by not shaking his hand when I introduced them. I hadn't realized that had happened and apologized for not "sticking up" for him. That was obviously not enough. He calmed down while we were out, but the moment we got into my house Richard wouldn't let it go. We spent hours talking about how upset he was; I was crying and just wanted it to stop.

17

I laid in bed that morning thinking about what had happened. I felt like I'd done something really wrong, but at the same time, I also felt like this may be a sign to break it off with him. If he could get so upset over something like this, maybe I shouldn't continue the relationship. I also already had feelings for him which were clouding my judgment. A couple of days later, Richard asked me to go see a movie. I accepted. Although I'd seen what felt like a red flag, I thought that since I hadn't been in the healthiest relationship before, maybe he had good reason to be upset. Maybe it was my reaction that wasn't appropriate. He also made sure to remind me that maybe I didn't have an appropriate response because of past relationships. Richard learned early how to use information in his favor.

Against my better judgment, I decided to forgive him and move on. I thought I was ready to be in a healthier relationship. I thought maybe my thinking was wrong, and I needed to get help from someone who cared about me. The sad part is that was true - but it wasn't him. I should have gotten help outside of the relationship before I allowed myself to date again.

It's hard to remember the exact order of all the horrible things that happened after that. There are moments that are so clear while most of them feel like a dream. Dating Richard was like a roller coaster ride. Things would be so amazing and then go south out of the blue. One time, he caused a scene at a friend's wedding. He left me at a restaurant and went back to confront a friend of mine and tell her it was my fault. She stood there listening not knowing what to do. Slowly, crazy became the new normal. I got used to him losing his temper and overreacting easily. I still wasn't aware of what was considered healthy! After the blow up things would get better again, just like when I was a kid.

One Friday night, he left me on the roadside after his nephew's birthday party. He threatened if I didn't "shut the fuck up" he would pull over and push me out of the car. I didn't stop talking. He didn't like that I was "talking back" so he pulled into a gas station and kicked me out. As he drove away, I kicked his car, leaving a huge dent in it. I felt bad for losing my temper, but I was so angry! I called a friend to come get me and I spent the night at her apartment. Richard tried to defend himself, saying it's because he didn't want to talk to me anymore and I wouldn't shut up. It was his way of "controlling the situation." According to him, the whole ordeal was all my fault because I was the one who lost my temper and kicked his car. Richard could not admit he'd threatened my safety. I let myself believe that. I was not yet aware of gaslighting.

Another night he woke me up at midnight on a weeknight because he wanted me to clean out the junk drawer. I told him everyone had a junk drawer in the kitchen and I would look at it later. Richard kept turning the lights on and pulling the sheets off of me until I got out of bed. He then proceeded to dump the drawer all over the floor. I cried as I picked everything up and put it back in the drawer.

When he asked me to marry him, a year after we started dating, it should have been obvious for me to say no. He took me to Oheka Castle on my birthday and planned a very beautiful weekend. Richard proposed in the French gardens of the Castle, which is a luxurious, beautiful place in Long Island. I had my reservations, but I was also spellbound. I thought it was normal for a relationship to have serious problems. I was also used to anger issues because my father had them. I told myself that it wasn't like that all the time and deceived myself into thinking I could make it better. After all, a friend had reminded me, "You are going to have to deal with shit, just depends on whose you choose." I was 29 and thought if I wanted a chance at having a marriage and a family, I should stop being so picky. Twenty-nine felt so old at the time! I said yes, and we celebrated our engagement with some of our good friends. That weekend I felt like the possibilities of a good future were endless.

"Being Loved Shouldn't Hurt"

The Gardens at Oheka Castle Huntington, NY

As we prepared for the wedding, more red flags started popping up. It's amazing what you will ignore in trying to do what you think you are "supposed" to do. I wanted to have a small, intimate wedding on the beach with my family, either in North Carolina or on an island somewhere. Richard wanted to have a huge fancy wedding on Long Island. He'd get so angry when I would try to bring up what I wanted, so we did what he wanted. I chose to get married at the Castle where he proposed. If I couldn't get the destination and size I wanted, I wasn't going to compromise on the location!

Stephanie McPhail

I can't complain; it was like a fairytale! I tried to stay positive, thinking of the gorgeous place we would be saying our vows. There was definitely tension as we were preparing, but everyone assured me it was normal to be stressed while planning a wedding. I wanted so badly to believe them.

We got married eight months after he proposed, at the end of August. That day was one of the happiest days of my life. Everything felt perfect, the day was amazing, and I was overjoyed getting to see so many people I loved to come from all over to celebrate our day with us. My heart felt so full and hopeful. The day went by quickly and after saying our last goodbyes, we went back to the Castle where some of our friends were staying. We played pool and chatted about how beautiful the day was. Then my new husband made a comment about getting up to our honeymoon suite. I wasn't going to say no to that! We had such a luxurious room! There wasn't anything missing from the suite. It had a master bedroom with a four post bed and an extravagant mattress and pillows (made only for the Castle), another smaller bedroom, a kitchen, living room decorated in old French Victorian style, and a massive bathroom filled with mirrors, marble, and gold. It felt surreal.

"Being Loved Shouldn't Hurt"

Suite at Oheka Castle, bed was on opposite wall then- but you get the idea!

The most amazing day of my life was followed by a nightmarish night. We got into the honeymoon suite where Richard went straight to the beautiful marbled bathroom to run us a bath. My heart filled with anticipation of the magical night we'd have on our first night as a married couple. As the tub filled, we kissed and talked about the day. I asked him to help me take my dress off because it was a corset. I'd pictured many times how sexy it would be for him to unlace me like a present on our wedding night. Instead, he unlaced me nonchalantly as the water kept filling the tub.

I stepped out of the dress and put my foot in the tub, causing a small amount of water to spill out onto the floor. Now, picture a very deep tub in a large, beautiful, golden-mirrored, marbled bathroom with a drain in the middle of the tiled floor. The moment it happened, Richard immediately got upset and said he knew the owner and I had to be more careful. I said, "Sweetheart, there's a drain in the floor and I'm sure water spills out all the time; relax and let's enjoy this." Richard didn't relax. He got angrier with me for telling him to relax. He told me I didn't understand, I never cared about anything, and I was going to make him look bad. I said, "Please don't ruin the night by starting an argument about this." I asked him to take a breath, walk away, and let's start over. I was desperately trying to stop the situation from escalating, this was my new husband and it was our wedding night!

It was too late. I pleaded for him to calm down. That was the wrong thing to do. Richard got angrier. I was crying and begging him to stop. He was getting worse with everything I said. The light had gone out of his eyes and I could only see darkness in them.

I tried to remove myself, locking myself in the smaller bedroom with my body pushed up against the door and my heart pounding in my chest. I was scared. He banged on the door and told me to let him in. I was still hoping he'd realize his error and told him that if he calmed down I would let him in, but he wouldn't stop.

Richard kept banging, yelling that I was making a scene and I needed to stop hiding. I finally came out. He still had darkness in his eyes as he told me he wished he could throw me out the window. He threw his wedding ring across the room and told me he wished I would die. He went on to say the marriage was a mistake and that all of this was my fault. I kept asking him to stop, but he kept following me and yelling.

I was still naked. In my mind, I wanted so badly to go outside into the hallway to get away from him, but I was embarrassed that I had no clothes on. What would the people he worked with think if they saw me? I was more worried about him and his name then I was about my own safety!

Richard followed me into the bedroom, pushing me onto my back on our beautiful king size plush bed. He put his hands around my neck and started squeezing. I was fighting, telling him to get off of me and to stop what he was doing, but he just kept squeezing harder until I started to feel my limbs get heavy. I thought I may actually die on my wedding night. I stopped fighting; the person that was supposed to love me was going to kill me. Tears streamed down my face. As I gave up, it was like Richard "came to" and saw me again. The darkness went out of his eyes and a look of sadness overcame them. He climbed off of me and walked slowly away.

By this time it was almost 4:30 in the morning. We'd gone up to our suite around 12:30 am. I curled up in a ball and just cried. I thought about all of the people who'd traveled all the way to my wedding. I thought of how embarrassed I was that I'd gotten married to this man and knew it was a mistake. I thought about what I was going to do to get away. I was so overwhelmingly sad, my body ached.

Richard came back with his head hung down, asking if we could talk. I told him I didn't want to talk and it was over; he'd crossed the line to a place we could never move past. He begged and pleaded for me to forgive him, reminding me of our guests who had come and the money we'd spent. He told me he'd gotten us a helicopter ride for our honeymoon. Our car to the airport was picking us up in only an hour or so. Richard promised if things weren't wonderful on the honeymoon, I could end the marriage and he wouldn't fight it. He also promised none of this would ever happen again, saying he was shocked at his behavior. Lots of words. He'd always been a very good salesman. His apologies were with tear-filled eyes and what looked like a genuine yearning to change. I told him it'd take a while and he had to be ready for me to be angry. I wanted so badly to find a way to make all of this better, to make it okay.

Richard agreed to do whatever it took for me to feel safe and secure again, so I finally agreed to go. I'd gotten no sleep, and as we got into the limo, I felt like I was dead. I felt so empty and sad and angry and disappointed. I barely spoke to him until we arrived in the Dominican Republic. We were escorted to a helicopter that took us on a ride over the towns, villages, and beautiful crystal blue ocean water. He told me to sit in front so I could get a better view; it was amazing. All the while he was quiet, almost sheepish, and seemed to feel bad for his behavior. We were away for a total of four days, and it took two of them for me to finally start to relax a little bit and try to enjoy the honeymoon.

A few months went by, and I started to feel less anxious. Things were good; I was happy. Trying to forget what happened on our wedding night, I started to feel comfortable that it really wouldn't happen again. But of course, if that were the case, I wouldn't be writing this book! About a week before Halloween, we were invited to a party. Richard got angry with me because someone he didn't like had been invited and was going. He yelled, called me names (his favorites were always CUNT, BITCH, and WHORE) threatened me, and then went into our living room and started throwing furniture. Then he drove away.

Some friends arrived five minutes later to head to the party. I wiped my tears and got ready to pretend everything was okay. They gave me a hug, told me how cute I looked, and then asked me how I was doing and where my husband was. I started to cry. I told them what had just happened. I wasn't sure what to do, but

I didn't want to ruin anybody else's time. I decided to go to the party and try to have fun.

Richard texted and called me the entire time. I came home a few hours later, and he apologized for losing his temper. I thought, now he's back to this kind of behavior. I felt devastated and angry at myself for being in this relationship and not ending it when I should have. I didn't tell anyone else what was really going on. I'd heard a lot of people say the first year of marriage was always the hardest. They had no comprehension of what I was dealing with at home. As in times past, part of me hoped it was just us "getting to know each other."

I felt like I was doing everything I could to make things better. I'd try to placate him and became constantly worried I was doing something wrong, I felt like I was always walking on eggshells. I agonized over what he would say or do. I'd think about how he'd react so that I wouldn't make him angry. Trying to do whatever I thought would make him happy, I felt more and more unhappy and nervous. About a year and a half into our marriage, I felt myself changing for the worse.

We went to Las Vegas to visit a friend. The first night we got there he said he wanted to show me the old and new strip. i was excited because I had never been. As the night went on and more alcohol was had he suddenly told me that I didn't seem excited enough that I was there and left me, by myself with no hotel key in the streets of Vegas! I had no idea where I was and did my best to find my way back to the hotel where he wasn't in our room. I went back towards the front desk to find him angrily walking towards me.   I screamed at him, what the hell was wrong with him for leaving me by myself in the city. Richard barely said a word and almost slammed the door as I tried to get into the hotel room. He proceeded to call me a stupid cunt and get in my face and told me I wasn't welcome to stay at the hotel with him anymore. I told him it was fine, I went to grab my things and get the cash I had brought-almost one thousand dollars- and it was gone! I asked him where it was and he told me I couldn't have it. I told him I had no problem going somewhere else if he gave me the money back but he refused.   My identification was in his wallet so I literally had nothing. I tried to suppress my anger and got into the other bed in the room. He proceeded to keep pulling my sheets off and pretended to call the police and tell them he wanted me removed from the room. My heart was pounding in my chest. I didn't know where to go so I just clutched the sheets and begged him to stop so I could go to sleep.

When I woke up the next morning I tried to look for my identification and money but still couldn't find it. He had hidden it. I took my clothes and went to the pool to try and clear my head. When I went back to the room he was awake and his normal apologetic self after an outburst. Richard told me the reason why he had lost his temper so badly was that he was going through withdrawals from pain medication he was abusing needed my help. For some reason, in my mind, this gave a reason for his irrational behavior.

He agreed to go to couple counseling with me. Therapy was so uncomfortable. There were several occasions where the therapist asked him to leave the session and told me I needed to get out. Richard would leave most sessions angrier. It got to a point where our therapist refused to continue seeing us because he was so volatile. She recommended I see someone on my own to understand why I was putting up with his behavior.

Not long after that, there was another event where he spit on me, got in my face and raised his fist to punch me but refrained, I kicked him out of the house. He actually left. I hoped that his time away would make him realize that his behavior wasn't going to stand with me. I hoped he'd start to make the changes he needed to make in order for our relationship to be healthy and less volatile. Richard promised to go to a therapist. He admitted that in the first year of our marriage when he wouldn't come to bed, he'd developed a cocaine problem that he'd hid from me. He had a long history of using pills, and other drugs, and explained that he was in an unhappy place. He was using that to cope. Being the crisis counselor/empath, I automatically went into caretaker mode. I didn't think about myself or how it was affecting my life. I wanted to help him get better because I'd promised to be married to him and spend the rest of my life with him. I felt like it was my responsibility to help him through his issues. Richard's excuses for why he had been abusive gave me hope that change was possible if I just supported him enough.

After a few months, I let him move back into the house and things were different for a while. Then he secretly stopped going to his therapist. I could tell he wasn't going to therapy because he would become more volatile. It was like that one hour a week had been a release for him. When I called him out for not going, he admitted it, saying he was better and didn't need to go anymore. I noticed a major difference in his behavior and reminded him the only reason I'd allowed him back into the house was upon his promise that he'd go to therapy. Of course, this made him angry and he refused to go back.

Time continued to pass; we would have really great days, sometimes weeks! When we were connected, it was hard for it to be much better. Then things would get bad. I felt crazy and questioned what I was doing wrong. I felt that there had to be something wrong with me, that I was causing him to behave this way. Richard often muttered under his breath that I was talking too loud, or embarrassing him. He was good at manipulating me to feel that I was responsible for his behavior.

I was 31 and felt like this was just going to be my life. For some reason at that time, 31 felt so old; I felt past my prime and afraid to start over again. I felt like I needed to try everything to make things work.

Eventually, we had another big blowout, and I had to get the police involved. After he spit on me again in the living room and threatened me, I escaped into our bedroom and locked the door. I had my dresser shoved against the door, pushing against it with my legs so he couldn't open the door. He kept banging on the door and trying to push his body weight into it until it cracked. Once he got in, Richard told me we should have sex and attempted to pull my pants down. He tried to block my ability to leave but I ran around him, telling him to stay away from me. I made it to my car and drove off. My heart was pounding in my chest. He followed me. I went straight to the police station and pressed charges. This was my first order of protection against him.

He spent almost a week in jail. He and his family kept telling me he was going to lose his job and it would be my fault. They refused to see it was due to his behavior. I felt guilty and took money out of my retirement savings to pay his $10,000 bail.

We weren't allowed to see each other due to the order of protection. I guess that made it more enticing to both of us because there were a few times we met up when we weren't supposed to see or contact each other. The dysfunction was like a drug: you know it's bad, but you keep going back.

He moved out for the second time and got an apartment. If I was someone watching everything from the outside in, it would've been obvious that I needed to leave him, but it's not always so cut and dry when you are dealing with it daily. Crazy was my normal!

While he was gone, he seemed like he was working through his issues and seemed to be much happier than I had ever seen him. I started to have hope again that the good part of him had gotten stronger. After a few months, I started to really miss him because I was watching him be happy and do positive things for himself. I was the one who begged and pleaded for him to come back. I felt like I'd been put through so much that I deserved to be with the improved version of him.

I took him a bottle of champagne as a sign of peace and we talked about how we could possibly save our marriage. Richard was actually the one who said he wasn't sure. I said, "Well if things are this good now, we could really have a great life together." He told me that the reason he'd been so angry was that of how much he hated his job. He had to go to work six days a week and was feeling so frustrated at work, he was taking it out on me. If he could go to school full-time instead of part-time and work somewhere he enjoyed, he'd be able to change. My heart full of hope and with my last hurrah, I allowed him to move back into our home.

Before this conversation, I'd started talking to a guy I'd had a crush on in college. We had planned to meet up for a drink before I allowed my ex to move back in. I think part of me was looking for someone to be interested in saving me. I wanted so badly to feel like a "good guy" would be interested in me (instead of being my own savior). My ex found out. I was doing volunteer work and got an angry message that I was a cheater and a liar. Nothing had happened! How did he find out? Richard had been going through my cell phone and had read through all of my old conversations.

This was another huge red flag, not that I ignored it necessarily, but I still tried to placate him. My instant response was, "Then don't move back in. I'm not interested in starting out your last chance with an issue. If you're going to stay stuck here and not be able to move on then you shouldn't move back in." I was half hoping he'd make the decision for me and not come back! We fought for more than two weeks. It was a big ordeal for me trying to help him make sense of things and him calling me a whore. He called the guy and harassed him on top of it. I was once again embarrassed. Even with everything this man had ever done to me, I still had never cheated on him. I was loyal and I was committed to trying to make things work.

I let him move back in. He got a job at a local restaurant as a waiter and signed up for school full-time. It didn't take long for things to get bad again. There comes a point where lines have been crossed so many times that respect doesn't exist. I stopped wanting to come home to deal with him and spent a lot of time with my best friend. Richard accused me of being a lesbian and kept telling me I was a cheater. I'd gotten to a point where just seeing his car in the driveway gave me anxiety. I'd be happy all day at work and I'd be happy with my friends, then I'd come home to him in a bad mood. I felt like I was walking on eggshells all the time. It's hard to be happy when you are afraid to totally be yourself.

When he moved back in, he'd promised to pay $500 towards the bills every month. Within three months, he was no longer paying anything. When I asked Richard for money or would try to bring it up, he'd lose his temper. In order to keep the peace, I stopped asking him for money. I got more and more in debt.

Richard would complain that I wasn't working enough extra hours to help support him as he was going back to school. I was working as a bartender a few days a week as well as extra hours at my regular job to try to make sure that I could pay my bills.

One night, as I was sleeping, he suddenly flipped the light on and jerked the sheets off of me. I was so scared, my heart was pounding in my chest, I had no idea what was happening. His face was directly on mine, screaming. I told him to get out of the room, and I pushed his face away from mine in an attempt to defend myself. Richard called the police. When they arrived, he told them I'd abused him, and he wanted me out of the house. They took a look around, saw that I was calm, and asked whose name was on the house deed. When I let them know it was mine, they asked me what I wanted to do. I told them he needed to leave; I was just trying to sleep. I also let them know he had psychiatric issues, and I had no idea what was going on with him. They asked him to leave and he left, for a little bit. This became a common occurrence.

I knew I needed to get away but also wanted to make sure I had enough money saved. I also needed to mentally prepare myself for the fight I knew was coming once I told him I was done.

Things only got worse. Another night after having a nice night out with friends, we got home and started arguing. We had a hallway that separated the kitchen and the bedroom. I wanted to get away from him but he wouldn't let me through and ended up pushing me. The force was strong enough that I fell on the ground and banged my head on the tile floor. Luckily, it didn't knock me out, but when I got up I just held my head, stared at him, and walked away with tear-filled eyes. I didn't want to be home. Being around him made me feel nervous and uncomfortable. I looked for any excuse not to be around him.

On Saturday, May 5th, things changed. I'd gotten up early to go to one of my extra jobs. He told me he expected to make at least $500 waiting tables that day. I was strangely hopeful that meant I'd be getting some money to help pay for bills. I left for work and about two hours later got a text message that said he'd quit his job. My first reaction was to ask him to go back and apologize for losing his temper; we both needed the money that day was going to bring! Richard's response was, "Just like TYPICAL CUNT BITCH Stephanie to not support her husband." Reading those words screamed loud in my head as I thought of how selfish and untrue they were. I'd done nothing but be helpful, even hurting myself, for him to have the opportunity to create the life he wanted! Here I was working extra hours to make money for the house, being yelled and cursed at, threatened, while being put down for everything I did, and this was the thanks that I got? In that very moment, the last ties to the relationship were cut. I couldn't imagine being with someone who'd treat me that way for the rest of my life. I knew it was time to make changes.

After work, I went to a shooting range with a friend of mine (a great way to blow off steam!). He reminded me what it would be like to feel special again. I felt stronger already with that reminder and the knowledge I could end things and it would be okay. I thought about how I was going to end this awful marriage as quickly and painlessly as possible. I also knew I had to be worried about my safety because I never knew how he'd react to hearing that I was once again ending our marriage.

When I got home, the whole drama started again, and I blurted out that I wanted a divorce. In the past, I would've listened to him asking for forgiveness and promising he would change. This was the first time I had no interest whatsoever in getting back with him, no matter what he said or did. I was finally done. It was a relief; it's like I'd cut off that attachment that I had with him. It was totally gone.

A week prior to this incident, I'd seen a friend I've known since elementary school. We are still friends but don't see each other often. I admitted to her that things were going badly at home and that I had nowhere to go. She offered for me to stay at her house. I let her know Richard was a loose cannon and I wasn't sure what he was capable of, but she assured me that he wouldn't figure out where she lived. Even if he did, her entire house was monitored, and she had no problem calling the police at any sign of him. She was the first person I called that night. All I said was, "Is the offer still open?" She said "Yes." I let her know I planned on moving in the next few days. I was afraid to say much more because I wasn't sure if he was listening and didn't want to send messages because I knew he looked through my cell phone.

I immediately started the divorce process and of course, it took time. It wasn't pretty, just as I had thought. There strangely seemed to be men coming out of the woodwork. I was admittedly enjoying some of the attention because it'd been so bad for so long, it was nice to just feel attractive again.

The bad part was that the guy I'd tried to meet up with when Richard and I were on a break became a part of the new drama. Richard found out that we were hanging out again and, of course, called and threatened him, telling him I had an STD. He successfully scared that prospect off, along with the next few people that I even showed a slight interest in.

It was like clockwork: he would find out that I was dating someone and would call them to tell them that I had an STD or that we were working things out. The guy would then stop calling me. Even so, I didn't give up. I knew that even if I never was with anyone again, I didn't have to live with Richard anymore and I didn't have to go home to him. That gave me strength.

I lived at my friend's house for three months while he lived in my house. At first, he didn't want to leave. We'd done the back and forth so many times, I'm sure he thought I'd forgive him and things would go back to normal. Richard finally realized I was serious about not wanting him back. He was worried he wouldn't have the money to move out so I sold my engagement ring and wedding band to give him money for the down payment for a rental. I knew that the money really belonged to me, but I was willing to do anything to get him out of the house as quickly as I could.

When I was finally able to move back into the house, I felt such a relief while at the same time feeling a slight sadness because it was just me and my dogs. I wasn't very comfortable living completely by myself, and I knew that life would be much more comfortable if I had a housemate. Within a week, someone I knew introduced me to a guy who was much younger than me and not in my circle of friends. He was the perfect candidate for a housemate, and he moved in.

Two weeks later, a friend of mine I used to work with asked me to meet up. She was in town, and I hadn't seen her in a while. I told her I'd love to have her over so we could catch up. The morning of that day, I got a message from her that she no longer wanted to come over and instead wanted to meet up with another friend and me more than 30 minutes away. Instead of following my gut instinct and saying no, I agreed. We started off the day by going to see the movie Magic Mike, which I also didn't want to see, but I figured I'd just go and not complain.

Here I was, going to see a movie that I didn't want to see, going to a place I didn't want to go, and pretty much doing nothing I wanted to do on a cold rainy night in July (when normally it's hot outside). All of those should have been my warning signs.

After the movie, my friends and I went out. We had two drinks in the first place, two glasses of wine at the next place, and then at the last place I ended up running into someone I knew who happened to be the bartender. He kept offering me free shots. I kept telling him no because I'd have to drive at some point, so I gave the shots to other people at the bar. The friends I was allegedly there to see talked to each other and basically ignored my other friend and me, to the point where we finally said we had to go.

We said our goodbyes and went to another place. I thought we'd be there for a while, so I ordered us both drinks. I was so excited to be out - I really wanted to have a good time. My friend went to the bathroom and when she came out she seemed angry. She was talking about leaving. I let her know I'd just gotten us drinks (they weren't cheap at this place!). She made a comment about how if I was so concerned about money then she'd just pay me back for it. I didn't want to seem cheap, but I also hated wasting money, so I quickly downed my whole drink. I wish I could go back on that decision!

We got back to her place, where my car was, and she slammed the door without looking back. I was drunk. There was no doubt in my mind I was drunk, but I didn't know what to do. She didn't invite me in, and I didn't ask. Instead, I sat in my car thinking about how much I wanted to get home and how much I didn't want to drive. Had I not been drinking, I'd have thought things through better. After a few minutes, I started up the car and started to drive. I was so uncomfortable and worried, I immediately pulled into a gas station next to my friend's road and turned off the car. I sat there for a few minutes, thinking about what I was going to do. I knew I didn't want to drive home but couldn't think of any other options. My best friend and my housemate were both away, and any of my friends that were close had kids and couldn't come and get me (this was before Uber). I started getting cold, so I turned the engine back on for heat. At that point, I figured I'd just drink my bottle of water and eat the snacks I had in my car, possibly walk to 7-11 and get more water, and just wait it out until I felt okay to drive. My plan didn't work out.

I'm not sure how long I had sat in my car with my eyes closed, head on the headrest, listening to music when all of a sudden I heard a knock on my window. I was scared for a second until I realized it was a police officer. I waved him off saying I was okay but he asked me to open my window. I complied and he immediately asked for my license and registration. I couldn't find it. As I was searching, I realized there were other officers around my car with flashlights. I gave the officer what I could and he asked me to step outside. At this point, I still didn't think anything bad was going to happen. I wasn't driving and was trying to do the right thing, in my mind, so I didn't think twice. I did what I was told. He started to give me a sobriety test; I knew I was in no shape for it. He asked if I'd been drinking, and I said yes and because of that, I didn't want to drive. He asked me if I'd do a breathalyzer and I knew I wouldn't pass, so I said no. Next thing I knew, I had handcuffs on me and was being put in a cop car.

I was taken to the police station. I was immediately handcuffed to a table in front of a window where a police officer asked me questions and made me fill out paperwork. I was still in shock! This couldn't be happening to me! I was taken in and photographed. Even when you're being arrested, it's hard not to smile when you know a picture is being taken. They make you take out anything that's holding your hair back; now I understand why people always look a little extra crazed in their mugshots!

My Mugshot!

"Being Loved Shouldn't Hurt"

The officers were asking me to do a breathalyzer, and I was trying to hold off as long as I possibly could. I knew I was way over the limit and at this point the lower it was the better. I was hoping enough time would go by that the number would decrease. They let me call anyone and everyone that I thought I may need to call. After several unanswered phone calls I finally, reluctantly, called my ex-husband. I knew there was a good chance he'd use this against me, but I'd run out of choices. I had no family near me to help and I needed to know that someone would be there to get me in the morning. He answered and started yelling at first. I spoke over the yelling and explained what had happened. He hung up angrily but called back a few minutes later, saying he'd be there in the morning with a lawyer.

I couldn't put off the breathalyzer anymore; it was either blow or lose my license for a year. I blew a 2.2 - almost three times the legal limit! I was taken to the back where I had to remove my shoes and take off my clothes to be searched. I wanted to cry and run. I couldn't. It was so demoralizing. I was taken to a small individual cell (luckily) about the size of a closet with a bathroom next to the bench. I laid on the bench trying to will myself to sleep, repeating "this too shall pass" as I pulled my arms into my shirt for warmth. I was afraid to ask for a blanket. Hours crept by as I stared at the bars and the dirty toilet not far from my face.

Stephanie McPhail

It was time to be transported to court. I was called to the front of my cell, my hands and feet were shackled, and I had to follow the chain gang into a large van where a few of us were attached together inside. There were no windows, so we had no idea where we were going. We weren't allowed to talk to each other the entire time; I'm not sure I even wanted to.

We were unloaded and lined up against a wall, where we stood as the cuffs were taken off of us. One of the police officers was letting his "power" get to his head and was definitely going out of the way to be nasty. I'm sure he was trying to push people to get a rise out of them. We were then led to a large holding cell where we sat for about 45 minutes, then moved to another larger cell where other people were brought in. One girl kept saying she hadn't done anything wrong and it was her boyfriend that had put his hands on her, another girl was going through really bad detox next to me, and the nasty cop kept walking by and throwing paper and garbage at her as she rocked and held herself on the bench. I realized at that moment I hadn't gone to the bathroom in hours. I couldn't hold it anymore, and the girl who said she was hit by her boyfriend offered to watch the cell as I went to the bathroom. It's a very strange feeling to be locked up in a room with other people you don't know without the ability to leave.

"Being Loved Shouldn't Hurt"

There was a family of women there, the oldest woman looked me straight in the eyes and said, "Don't worry sweetheart, it's all going to be okay." It gave me the tiniest bit of relief. I was someone who'd only had detention once in my life, and here I was sitting in a room with bars.

My name was finally called. It was around 7:30 am on a Saturday. I was given very specific instructions about how to leave the cell: don't look around, don't talk, and follow the yellow line until we are told to stop and then wait to be called. My name was next.

I'd never felt so relieved to see my ex-husband as I was that morning with my divorce lawyer behind him. I was told where to stand while the judge asked me some questions as my lawyer came up to the podium to speak for me. Everything was a bit of blur; I was happy someone else was talking because I was at a loss for words. Suddenly, I was told I could leave and I walked as quickly as I could to my ex with my lawyer following close behind. He was telling me I wasn't allowed to drive and he'd be letting me know what the next steps were in a few days.

I sat in the car without saying much. There wasn't anything to say except yes or no to my ex and just listen to whatever he had to say. I didn't feel like I had much of a leg to stand on, now that I'd been in jail myself. Richard drove me to my house where I sat on the couch and stared at my television without actually seeing the images. I didn't want to talk to anyone, except to call someone to bring my car back.

The next few months were a blur of going to different drug and alcohol counselors for observation, regular visits to DMV with a lot of money spent to just be allowed to drive to work and doctor/counseling visits, trips to my lawyer's office, the court, and some "help" from my ex. Richard was trying to use my legal issues to start a relationship with me again. Although I appreciated the help in getting from Point A to Point B, there was no way I'd ever start another relationship with him. I was more than happy to keep a friendship, especially because I needed help, but he kept trying.

I started to date again. My ex was partially supportive of it; every once in a while he'd get angry and scream at me, then tell me later he understood why I wanted to date. The fact that I didn't live with him anymore made the tantrums bearable because I didn't have to go back home with him. I told myself I could handle that kind of relationship with him. I really needed his help, so I was willing to deal with his sudden outbursts.

At this point, almost a year had passed. I was still going through all of my legal issues in court, but nothing had been finalized. I felt so embarrassed when I told dates I'd been arrested. At the end of June, as I was scrolling through dating profiles, I stopped on a guy that I recognized from junior high and high school. We had actually dated in 7th grade! He'd always stuck in my mind for some reason. I wrote him a message and he quickly called me on the phone. He seemed so nervous to talk to me, it felt really sweet. I thought it was so cool that he was a musician and that he lived part-time in Maui, Hawaii. Guitar Guy lived a carefree life with pretty much the clothes on his back and a few items in his bag.

I have never in my life, even to this day, felt the kind of connection and energy with anyone that I felt with him. From our first date, the energy I felt from Guitar Guy was so overwhelming I could literally feel him pull into my driveway; I could feel his presence in my mind. It was so intense, but something was a little off. When he was there, I felt like I was buzzing with energy and excitement, which felt so good. However, when he left, I'd feel drained, exhausted, and sad. It was a strange feeling to experience.

Guitar Guy started to show a pattern of disappearing from all communication for days at a time. I was noticing that he wasn't very reliable. When I'd try to talk to him about it, he'd become very frustrated with me. What did I do? I accepted it for the kind of person he was. Things were so intense with us that in my mind, it had to mean I was making the right decision by being with him. Not to mention the sex was amazing! We started to make plans for the future: me possibly leaving my job, moving to Maui, him coming to France to meet my family. It was exciting to plan things with someone. We made out like teenagers; it was hard for us to keep our hands off of each other. Since Guitar Guy was so simple and different than anyone else I'd ever met, it felt exciting to look at the world in a different way. He was very "spiritual" and made me more aware of my spirituality, which I had lost connection with along the way.

I was totally honest about getting a DWI (Driving While Intoxicated), and it didn't seem to bother him. He'd take me upstate to hang out with his family, and we genuinely had a wonderful time together. I kept trying to see what I could do to be supportive of his need to "escape and make music," which was his excuse for not answering phone calls.

It was the beginning of September, and my time at court was coming to a close. The judge decided I'd be prosecuted to the fullest extent of the law. This meant I'd be on probation for the next three years and have a breathalyzer installed in my car. Having to endure the process of going to the police, then probation, and being watched and questioned for everything I did was starting to wear on me. I could feel the nerves starting to build up in my body.

"Being Loved Shouldn't Hurt"

Two days later, I found out my grandmother had passed away in France. She was my last grandparent and I'd been very close to her; I was devastated. I'd planned to visit her that December one last time. I took a few days off work to mourn my grandmother at home. I wanted to fly to France but decided not to go since everything would be over by then, and getting permission to go anywhere when you are on probation is extra difficult!

I was always someone who worked out a lot. It was and still is, a great coping mechanism I've used since I was a teenager. I'd gotten into Crossfit a few months earlier after looking for a way to get in shape for a girls trip to Miami.

It was now October, only two weeks had passed and stress was starting to be more constant. I attempted to burn off the anxious energy by working out more. After a particularly hard workout, we drove upstate to see my boyfriend's family. We had a great time. We even went to an amusement park and helped his family with the kids. The next day, I woke up to my left arm was being swollen to twice its size. I wasn't able to stretch it out straight.

My gut told me I needed to get to the hospital immediately. Once we were there, they took me in quickly for a sonogram. The technician took one look at me and said "I think you have a blood clot." I looked at him like he had two heads. I can't have a blood clot! I don't smoke, I eat well, and I exercise! After 30 minutes of looking all around my arm, he found it. A blood clot about two inches wide was keeping blood flow from reaching my arm. I was scared! The doctor told me I had to immediately go on blood thinners, stop working out, and had to basically sit on my couch for the next few weeks until the blood thinners had circulated my body.

I was stunned. Why? Why was this happening to me? We drove back to his family's house with my new medications and a look of shock on my face. During our drive home the next day, I told him how scared I was and how much I'd need his help to do basic things. I wasn't even able to pick up a bag of dog food. I wasn't allowed to drive anywhere except work and appointments. He said he understood and would come to help me whenever he could.

Three days went by. Although I'd spoken to him on the phone for a few minutes and we'd exchanged some text messages, I hadn't seen him. I tried getting him to come over, but Guitar Guy kept making excuses. I kept giving him the benefit of the doubt. I tried to understand that even though I was lonely and scared, other people still had to live their lives. If I didn't sit still and relax, there was a chance the blood clot could kill me! There's nothing much scarier than that to force you to analyze the time you've wasted!

"Being Loved Shouldn't Hurt"

You know who did check in? My ex-husband. Richard called me once a day to chat and see how I was doing. After a few days of my boyfriend not coming by, my ex went to the store for me. A few days later he called to ask if I'd been out of the house and since I hadn't, he came by to pick me up. He told me this guy wasn't right for me. It was hard to listen to my ex give any kind of relationship advice.

A few days later, my boyfriend finally wanted to make plans. I'd been home for more than a week and hadn't seen him once. I'd made plans with Richard, who wanted to get me out of the house. I wasn't going to drop those plans after I hadn't been a priority for Guitar Guy. I decided I'd still hang out with Richard and then I'd have him drop me off at my boyfriend's house; both men agreed that was okay. I explained to my boyfriend how hurt and scared I was and how much I really needed him around to help me. He made an offhand comment about me hanging out with my ex-husband, and I got upset with him. I'd asked him ahead of time, and he'd been okay with it. Besides, he wasn't coming himself to help me! We agreed from then on I wouldn't do anything with my ex alone.

A few weeks later, in November, my boyfriend was telling me about a well-known author, Graham Hancock, who was coming to NYC for a book launch. He'd been telling me about this author for a long time, so it was exciting to be able to hear him speak.

The day of the speaking event, he arrived at my house and, out of the blue, told me he'd spoken to his ex-girlfriend. She'd been feeling down, so he invited her to the city with us. I didn't even know he still spoke to his ex-girlfriend. I tried not to be jealous, since I'd recently spent time with my ex. I was conflicted immediately because I'd been VERY open. It seemed strange to me that she was just showing up out of nowhere. He assured me it was fine and we'd all get along.

The train ride in was awkward to say the least. Once in the city, we had to run to the location because we were late. It was standing room only. Guitar Guy stood behind me and held my hand, which helped alleviate some of the fear that was creeping up in my chest. When Graham Hancock was done speaking, we left, deciding to stop at a restaurant for food before we went home. I reminded them I had work in the morning and couldn't stay out for too long. I listened to them go back and forth like longtime friends. Listening to them, I also thought they were two of the most selfish people that I'd ever met. When we left, I invited her to come back to my house and sleep on the couch. I figured it was the nice thing to do for an old friend. We got back and stayed up for a while before I excused myself. It was after 1:00 am and I had to be up in five hours. My boyfriend came to bed with me. He said they were going to go back into the city tomorrow to look around since she'd never been to New York City. I agreed and said I'd come to meet them when I got off. It was a Friday before a long weekend, so I knew I'd get out of work early. After having some great sex, I felt reassured that the uneasy feeling in my gut might just be a little unneeded jealousy.

The next morning, Guitar Guy texted me to say they'd arrived safely. He let me know what the plans were and said I didn't need to come because they'd be home by the time I got there. We made plans to go out to dinner together, just the two of us, and for him to sleep over.

I went out with friends after work. Everyone got food except me, because I wanted to save room for dinner with my boyfriend. As the night went on, we had some drinks. I'd texted him a few times, asking for the approximate time of arrival at the train station. He finally texted back that they were walking to Penn Station and they'd be back soon. I was 5 minutes away, walking distance from the station, so I figured I'd meet them when they got back. Time kept passing, so I texted again. Now they'd stopped for a drink and were chatting. I asked if he knew an approximate time they'd be back - I was still waiting to eat with him. He told me I was being crazy, and he was going to turn off his phone if I didn't stop texting him! I begged him to please come back to my house when they returned, even if it was both of them. I had a horrible feeling in my stomach. Guitar Guy told me he'd had enough and was turning off his phone.

I felt so betrayed! I must really be stupid not to think something strange was going on, and now they were going back to his family's house to stay together. I was hurt, angry, and after not eating while I sat around thinking about my feelings, I was drunk. My friend offered to drive me home, and I agreed. I had a slight hope that I was wrong and that he'd show up at my house. He didn't.

I woke up the next morning with a headache and a huge pain in my chest. I must be wrong. I called, but he didn't answer. Later, I texted to see what was going on, and his response was that I was acting crazy. He needed a few days away to sort things out. I asked if he'd had sex with his ex. He assured me he hadn't and that I shouldn't be saying anything because I was friends with my ex. The day went on and I felt so confused. What was happening? Days passed and nothing. I was sick to my stomach; I couldn't breathe it hurt so badly. Everything that had gone on was running through my head, and I was questioning every single word I'd ever said to him. I tried to see where I might have messed up.

I decided to not try to contact him. This was extremely hard. Two weeks went by. We were supposed to go to his family's house for Thanksgiving.

"Being Loved Shouldn't Hurt"

I had no family close by and hadn't made other plans. I was waiting on him. I tried to contact him again; this time he said because I was acting so crazy and wasn't giving him the time he needed to clear his head, he didn't think it was a good idea for me to go. I'd given him two weeks with no contact! It was the day before a big holiday, and I was going to be alone. I called up a few friends and made plans with them instead.

The pain in my chest had become stronger than ever before. I couldn't eat because it just made me feel worse. I was obsessing over this man who'd "ghosted" me. I was a mess. After Thanksgiving, I started a routine of going to work then coming home and getting straight into my pajamas, putting on a self-help video, and staring at the screen for hours. The fragile relationship had been the only thing keeping me slightly afloat. Now that was gone, and I was alone. After everything I had been through, this was what finally put me over the edge. I felt hopeless.

I lost 20 pounds. Every day, I woke up feeling like my heart had been ripped out. I was so full of anxiety, it was hard to concentrate or do anything for myself. It even hurt to talk because it made me feel out of breath and light headed. I'd lay in bed, my chest feeling very tight, not able to sleep. I didn't interact with people because I couldn't bear to pretend I was okay or make small talk.

Stephanie McPhail

My ex kept showing up to help out. He started to make me feel bad because I gave him nothing in return. Remember, he's a good salesman, so he's good at getting what he wants. Richard basically wanted sex in return for all the help he'd given me. I felt so dead inside, it almost felt like it didn't matter. When we had sex, I felt like I wasn't even there; it was my body that was there but my mind wasn't there at all. After an "oops" night, I took the morning after pill. I was feeling awful, but I knew for sure that bringing a child into the mess of my life wasn't a good thing. When I finally told him I couldn't do it anymore, he got so angry that he threatened to call my probation officer and publicize my legal issues. The good thing about feeling like nothing matters is that this was also one of the things that didn't matter. I figured at this point, he could tell anyone anything, and I just didn't care anymore what people thought. I was having a hard time just getting up in the morning; this was the least of my worries.

Days passed slowly. I could feel every second tick by. Every moment I was obsessing over the guy that had disappeared. I felt so lost, hurt, and alone. I started doing yoga because it was the only thing that I was allowed to do with my medical condition. Yoga was also the only activity I could do that released the pressure from my chest and gave me a bit of a reprieve from the deep sadness enveloping me. I spoke to my best friend who told me to look for the lesson and went back to therapy. I wanted to look for the lesson and learn from my past, but I was so overwhelmed it was hard to even concentrate! I think part of me was angry and defensive, but I kept searching for something to keep me from spiraling even lower. What lessons could I possibly learn from all these horrible things that had happened to me?

She recommended the book *The Celestine Prophecy* by James Redfield, which talks about different types of relationships. There was a lot in there about energy. I learned from reading that book that the Guitar Guy who'd disappeared was an energy taker. He'd give me a whole bunch of energy, making me feel wonderful, and then he'd leave me high and dry. I'd feel drained.

Reading that book helped me start to look at things a little bit differently. I got tickets to see one of my favorite bands, Phish, and cried pretty much the entire show. I saw them again two days later for New Years with some friends and had a slightly different experience, but I still wasn't feeling very happy.

The new year came and it was time to go back to work. I woke up in the morning with my eye feeling itchy. I looked at myself in the mirror and it was red. I forced myself to go to work like I'd done so many times in recent months. Once at work, the itching got worse. I went to the nurse; she told me I had pink eye and had to go home. I went straight to the doctor for medication. I took the opportunity to get back to reading, even if it was only with one eye.

The next day I felt better and decided I needed to get back to work. During a break, I closed my eyes for a few minutes in my classroom. When I tried to stand up, my leg gave out, and I twisted my ankle. I laid on the floor trying to will the pain away. When I looked down, I saw what looked like a baseball sticking out of the side of my ankle. This wasn't a twist; it was a full fledged high-level sprain.

I didn't want to leave work. Within five minutes, my next set of students came in and my ankle was even more swollen. I kept teaching, pretending everything was okay like always. One of my students was so worried, he ran to the nurse. She advised me to go straight to the ER. Of course, the old contact information at work was for my ex-husband, so that's who they called. I let him know I was leaving and would meet him at the hospital.

Triage took one look at my ankle and took me in for x-rays immediately. Luckily, the emergency room wasn't busy that day and things went extra fast. I'd been in and out of hospitals way too many times in the past three months. As I was laying in yet another hospital bed, staring at my huge swollen throbbing ankle, I started to laugh and cry at the same time. All of the emotions I'd had in the past few months came over me. With tears in my eyes, I looked up and said out loud "I get it! I get it universe, things need to change! You've got my attention. I'm listening, and I need to fix this."

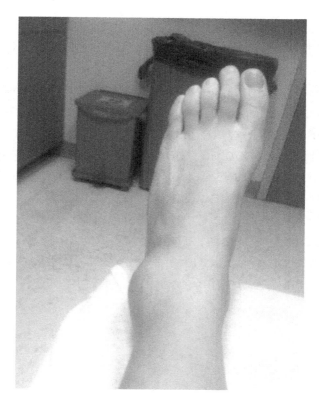

View of my ankle in the E.R.

I got home and went back to reading. I had plenty of time to sit around and was on the second book in a series. I finished reading the page I was on, turned it, and the next line was about the main character spraining their ankle! It went on to say that the sprain was due to not paying attention and could be healed by putting the correct energy in the right area. Wow, if this wasn't a sign that I was suddenly in alignment with the world around me, I don't know what was.

It's like a switch went off and things slowly started to change. I finally understood what "the universe" was throwing in my face. "YOU have the power to make life better! YOU are way stronger than you realize! Stop waiting around for someone else to come and save you; you have the power to save yourself! Stop hoping that someone else is going to change things for you and get out there and do it yourself! Stop feeling sorry for yourself; it could be worse!" All of these things resonated in my mind. For the first time in years, I felt my light and connection to the world come back, like a shade had been lifted and the sunlight was finally coming back in.

"Being Loved Shouldn't Hurt"

**Two weeks after my depression broke,
meeting Alex Grey-Famous Artist!**

I started to follow what made me feel good. There seemed to be a different energy, like the colors were brighter, when I was doing what made me happy. I really started focusing on my feelings, listening to what they were telling me. I'd done a lot of ignoring them before; I guess that's how I was trained from a young age. My own emotional wants and needs always seemed to be on the back burner to what everyone else needed. Not anymore. I stopped worrying about hurting people's feelings. Even awkward conversations I'd wanted to walk away from in the past, but hadn't, I started to walk away from.

I did a ton of reading and planning. I still had a breathalyzer in my car, I was still dealing with my legal issues, but I was going to take that as the lesson it was. I had to listen to my gut for once!

I'd always heard about float tanks. Since I'd started to live a "do what feels good now" life, I decided I wanted to try one out. There was one that had opened up in my area, and they were running a special. I was excited to try it out. If you haven't tried floating, imagine being in an area where there's no sound, no light, and your body feels weightless. It brought me to one of the deepest areas of meditation I'd ever felt. While I was floating, I saw a business I needed to create. A business that helped people overcome major obstacles and remind them to live their best version of life. I saw the different services I needed to include in the business to truly make it a whole health change. That's what I knew worked for me. I wanted to give back.

I left feeling renewed and inspired. I called the ladies that I'd seen in my "vision," and they agreed right away to be on board. We got together rather quickly and after a short dialogue, came up with the name "Mind and Body Awakenings" based on what I felt happened to me and what could happen for so many other people who needed it. I'd been "awakened" in my mind, body, and spirit, and now had the tools to help awaken other people to their full potential. Life was starting to get exciting, in a good way!

Around the same time, I found out my dad had a strange spot on his head. On further inspection, they found that he had skin cancer that may have spread to his brain. Emergency surgery was required. This would save his life but in order to remove all the cancer, they'd have to remove his right eye.

The "old me" would have let this overwhelm her and bring her back into depression. Not this time! Now, don't get me wrong, this sucked big time! However, I had a secure feeling that everything was going to be okay. It was hard to think how life would be for my father with one eye, but it was harder to think of life without him. He's far from a perfect man, but he's always been my rock. The surgery came and went. Although he was in a lot of pain, he was alive, and they were able to remove all the cancer cells.

With that hurdle crossed, I kept working on my business and started to VERY casually date again. I got back on the popular dating apps, but was bored by every date. I made a rule that I'd only go out for coffee. I could tell in the first second of meeting someone if I'd be interested; I didn't want to waste my time and energy staying longer than necessary.

Stephanie McPhail

One morning I checked my dating profile and had a message from a guy I'd contacted. He stood out because he was tall, dark, handsome, played rugby, and had moved to New York from Montana. Let's just call him Montana for short. He offered to drive over an hour to meet up with me. I figured, why not? If it's awful, at least I can leave and see my friends.

We met out in public, and he was even more handsome in real life than in his profile picture; that doesn't happen very often! Conversation was easy and we hit it off right away. I took him to local places I hung out in and a "hole in the wall" that I normally didn't frequent. That was his favorite since it reminded him of home.

I'd finally met a man who challenged me, in a good way. He was the perfect example of a gentleman: polite, genuine, upfront, very smart and all-around great guy. The downfall: he worked a lot and he was a hunter. As a vegetarian, I wasn't sure how I could work with something like that. There were so many other amazing things about him, I figured I'd stop trying to think of the future so much and go with what felt good now. We had so many things in common, and he was the first man I'd met who actually inspired me to continue working on me and push my comfort zone. It was refreshing.

"Being Loved Shouldn't Hurt"

It wasn't long before the phone calls started from my ex-husband. He called Montana at work and did his routine threats. I'd warned Montana it might happen. He let me know he wouldn't entertain calls like that in the slightest. If it happened again, he'd call the police. He admitted that people like that could be volatile, yet he wasn't saying he wanted to stop seeing me. Instead, he wanted to stick up for my honor and defend me. It was nice to feel wanted like that.

It was the first time that I saw what a genuinely good man looked like. I didn't have to walk on eggshells, and he brought out the best in me. Things were going very well. One day, after a trip to the beach, we started talking about a deer we saw. We went home and talked about the major difference in values we had. I wanted to save all the animals, and he saw animals as a way to sustain his family. This was going to be a big hurdle; we both knew it. When he left, he said he'd need some time to get his head straight. He admitted he had a wonderful time with me and was starting to think of the future with me. That brought up the reality that hunting would be a major issue in a future relationship. We both respected each other for our differences, but it would be difficult if we had children. He needed to think.

I gave Montana his time. A week went by, and I could sense he was having a really hard time with his decision. I spoke to people who I knew were in similar situations. How did they make it work? I tried to look at the issue from all sides. It wasn't long before I got a message saying he wanted to talk. I knew before even calling him back what he was going to say. I called back, trying to sound enthusiastic. He said that, after a lot of thinking, he decided that before feelings got stronger than they already were, he wanted to end the relationship. He didn't want either of us to go against our own values in order to be with each other. Montana knew if he went out hunting, I'd be home, upset he was hurting an animal. In turn, that would hurt him and possibly force him to change who he was. He didn't want either of us to grow resentful of each other over who we were. I told him I understood his decision even though it hurt, thanked him for being honest, and told him I was always around if he ever wanted to talk. He sounded sad when he ended the call.

After I hung up, I called a few of my friends to tell them we'd broken up. They were concerned I'd go back into my depression, but things were different for me now. I can't deny I was sad, but I truly felt he was missing out on a great person. However, I understood why he felt so strongly and actually, I respected him more for being so genuine. I thought how different my life would've been if I had met him earlier in my life. He showed me that a loving, committed relationship was possible - I'd just lived it. I'll always be grateful for that.

"Being Loved Shouldn't Hurt"

Following my passion led me to get flight lessons!

After that, I made a list. I'd never in my life known what I was looking for in a relationship. How could I know when I found the right person if I didn't know exactly what I wanted? The list was easy to make. It consisted of "Have to Haves," "Negotiables," and "Definitely Nots." As much as there were a lot of things similar to the man I'd just dated, there were definitely upgrades I needed in a "perfect" partner. If I was ever going to think about being in a long-term committed relationship again, I wasn't going to be stingy with my Wants. I was including it all this time around. In fact, as I started going on coffee dates with people, my list became more and more particular. The strange thing is that now the men that were attracted to me were mostly great guys, but they weren't what I was looking for.

As time passed, I learned a lot about myself; I learned a lot about who I was looking for and who I wasn't. Everyone has a different list, but here was some of mine: 6 ft 3, brown hair preferred but not necessary (even bald), spiritual, a musician, liked to travel, intellectual, in good shape/athletic, not into sports, someone I could bring to a party and not have to entertain him the whole time, not a huge fan of rap music, liked vegetables and open to eating vegetarian food, family-oriented, had used a drug or alcohol at some point in their lives but weren't daily users at this point, didn't have any children but wanted them, didn't live on Long Island, or at least wasn't born and raised here.

I was much less interested in dating at this point in my life, so I figured I could be picky. It was going to be hard to find everything I wanted, and that was completely okay with me. I was having such a great time being me; I wasn't ready for anyone else to come in and interfere with that. The next person I seriously dated would really have to show me how great they were!

I went to another Phish concert out of state and met up with a couple of friends of mine. While we were out in the field listening to music, I started to feel this very calm feeling flow through me. I remembered that with my exes, at concerts and activities, in those moments I'd feel anxious - like something was going to happen and I had to be cautious. Not this time. It was a nice feeling not having to worry that they were going to start fighting or there was going to be an issue. It finally clicked. I tugged on my friend's shirt and said, "I get it!" She looked at me for a second like I was nuts and said, "What do you get?" I said, "I finally get what love should feel like!" She smiled at me and asked, "And how is that?"

"Like this. Calm, peaceful, open, fun" I responded. It was the first time I actually felt it in my body, not just at an intellectual level.

Me at a Phish Show!

Everything was going great; I felt like I was on Cloud Nine! I watched the movie *The Secret Life of Walter Mitty*, a story about a man who disappeared into his own imagination. It was far from the best movie I've ever seen but it spoke to me. I was reminded that we could spend our whole lives not living the life we should, and what a waste it would be. I decided I needed adventure.

I called an adventurous friend, asking her if she wanted to drive cross country to Montana with me. I'd do all the driving. I would just ask her to pay for gas and tolls. I'd never been to Montana. It sounded so beautiful and different from home. She quickly agreed and the planning started right away. We didn't know each other well, but I knew she liked to travel and was reliable.

It got closer to the day of the trip, and I still didn't have full permission from my probation officer. I didn't give up. A week before we were supposed to go, a new breathalyzer was installed that was even harder to use than the last one. That wasn't going to stop me. The same day, my probation officer called me back to say he wasn't going to be able to let me go. It took a few days, but that no turned into a yes. The day of my departure arrived. I was starting the beginning part of my trip by myself; the first five days I'd be alone. I went to my probation officer to get my letter of permission for the trip. He was out of his office, and no one was willing to give it to me. I'd have to go to the court and try to speak to the judge. I got to court just as they were taking a recess. I spoke to a few people who said I couldn't speak to the judge until court was back in session. So I waited for 2.5 hours on a bench outside court, talking to whomever would listen to get me permission from the judge. Before I knew it, one of the men I'd spoken to about my trip came back with a big smile on his face and a letter in his hand telling me to have a great trip! I couldn't grab it quickly enough and left in a hurry. I was six hours off schedule, but I was on my way!

Stephanie McPhail

I could write a whole book on my travels, but for this book I'll keep out the details. My first stop was Hanover, Pennsylvania (the capital of snack foods). Then Chicago for their famous Chicago Pizza. Then to Iowa to see where "the music died." Next was South Dakota (my favorite!), where I met up with my friend. We went hiking and saw Mount Rushmore, The Black Hills, Needles Highway, The Badlands, Custer National Park, Sylvan Lake, and Sturgis during bike week. We then went to Yellowstone National Park in Wyoming, where we camped out for five nights and did a lot of hiking. We saw gorgeous wildlife and scenery. After that, we drove the long way up to Glacier National Park, as per Montana's suggestion, stopping on the way to see the highest highway in the US and the small little town he was from. We even got to hang out with the locals at the town fair, demolition derby, and bar! We had the time of our lives! We then started our drive back home, with the rain following close behind, through North Dakota and then Michigan and Wisconsin. We stayed in our tent in the rain but got to see Lake Michigan and its major waterfalls and lighthouse! We went back to Chicago for more pizza and the local sights. Then it was off to Pittsburgh, where we stayed with a friend of a friend who wanted to help us out in our adventure.

"Being Loved Shouldn't Hurt"

The Grotto of Redemption in a cornfield in Iowa

Stephanie McPhail

The Badlands of South Dakota

"Being Loved Shouldn't Hurt"

Wall Drug, South Dakota

Mt Rushmore, South Dakota

Stephanie McPhail

Devil's Tower, Wyoming

Meditating in Yellowstone National Park, Wyoming

"Being Loved Shouldn't Hurt"

Taking a break from our hike in Yellowstone National Park, Wyoming

After three weeks of a new adventure every day, it was finally time to make the last leg of the trip home. It was one of the best trips that I have ever been on. I felt so alive!

I was at the point where I finally felt happy to be single forever. I'd be able to go on any adventure without anyone trying to hold me back. I finally felt how much my past had been holding me back and knew I'd never let myself go back there again. Life was finally mine to decide how I wanted to live it! There had even been a point in the trip where my mom called to let me know about family drama. She wanted to get me involved, but I stood up for myself and refused to get sucked in. She wasn't happy with the new boundary I'd put up, and ended up not talking to me for a few months after that, but I had changed. Most people are not happy when new boundaries are put in place, but that's okay.

Before I'd left on my trip, I'd been seeing someone casually. While I was gone, he watched one of my dogs. It was pretty obvious that he was interested in me, but he wasn't fulfilling my list requirements. While I was on the trip, he asked if I was interested in going to a country music concert. I figured why not? I'd never been to a local country show. We had a great time. I'd known him for months, but hadn't progressed the relationship further than casual dates. That night, I explained to him I wasn't interested in a committed relationship. I just wanted to have fun doing whatever I wanted. If he wasn't okay with that, we'd have to remain platonic. Within a few days, we became more intimate. He was one of those men that was very good at finding out what I liked sexually and then teasing me with that exact information. It was a relief to have a "no strings attached" sexual relationship. It was completely different from what I'd experienced before. It was interesting because this guy was also a hunter. Since we weren't serious, that major difference in our values didn't bother him.

I knew The Hunter wasn't my dream guy and kept on my search because I knew settling was no longer an option. Life had become way too good for me to go backwards. I kept dating men from the dating apps and was always upfront and honest that it'd take a lot for me to stop being single. At that point, I really wasn't sure I was actually going to find anyone in this lifetime, and that was okay with me. I felt like dating was more for entertainment than for finding someone who I may want to spend the rest of my life with.

One day at the end of September, I was getting ready to go out with some friends and was going through dating profiles (I did this whenever I had downtime). I saw a guy with a beautiful smile, holding a guitar, and I was instantly excited to read his profile. My heart started beating a little faster when I read about him and realized he had everything on my list. I sent him a message telling him to read my profile because we seemed to have a lot in common. He replied pretty quickly and I suggested that we speak to each other on the phone. During my time dating, I'd come to the conclusion that if someone seemed even remotely interesting, it was important to talk on the phone quickly and meet soon to not waste any time with someone that wasn't a good match. We spoke, but it was a different phone call than I'd ever had. I immediately enjoyed the sound of his voice and for the first time in a long time, I felt like I didn't want to end the conversation. After about an hour (running late to meet my friends) I reluctantly said goodbye and we agreed if it wasn't too late when we got home we'd try to talk again before bed.

All night, I found myself thinking about a guy I'd never met. Recounting what we'd spoken about and how much I enjoyed the sound of his voice, I wanted to go home early so that I'd have time to talk to him again! I didn't want to seem needy so I didn't rush home too quickly, but I didn't stay as long as I would have. We spoke until early in the morning without even noticing the time pass. I let him know I had a date planned for Sunday but he said he wasn't worried. He asked to take me out to dinner in a week. Now of course this was against my "rules" but I didn't even question it. The Musician lived an hour and a half away and would come to Long Island during rush hour to come meet me. I was in.

We spoke a few times during the week; I already felt like we'd known each other a long time. I was excited for Friday to come, but I enjoyed the "getting to know" you conversations we were having. In what felt like the blink of an eye, Friday arrived. I'd been on enough dates to know that some people looked and sounded different in person, so as a backup, I asked a friend of mine to come out with me for a drink while I waited for my date to arrive. I wanted to make sure I had an easy excuse if he wasn't who he seemed to be.

He messaged me that he was parking his car and coming in, and I felt my heart rate increase in excitement. I stood at the bar and suddenly felt like I needed to turn around. As I did, I watched this gorgeous man walk in with what seemed like a glow about him. I had to catch my breath for a second and regain my composure when I realized it was my date! We started chatting and it felt like the rest of the world started to melt away. My friend noticed quickly and left, knowing I was in good hands. I felt comfortable and safe with him immediately.

After a few hours of chatting, dinner, and bar hopping, we shared a kiss. Not going to lie, I'd been staring at his lips for hours, hoping a kiss would be coming my way soon. I again had this sense of ease around him that was refreshing. He had such a good energy about him. Time passed quickly, and I knew he was in no shape to make the long trip back to his house. I offered him my couch if he promised not to try any "funny business". Of course, by the time we got to my place, I'd changed the offer to "girl cuddles" in my bed (which, amongst my friends and I, translates to actual cuddles, while "boy cuddles" is what guys say when they really mean they want sex). Although I think we both really wanted more than that, he accepted and didn't try to get me to change my mind.

The next morning I woke up to my ex-husband banging on the door. Richard had offered to drive me to our friend's birthday party and, because he knew I had a date, he'd decided to show up early. I was so embarrassed. I explained to The Musician it was my ex and opened the door to a very agitated man. I told him to leave and not worry about driving me anymore if he was going to behave like this. I don't know why I kept thinking he'd be respectful of me and my feelings if we were friends. I shut the door on him and he left. I walked back to my room to find my date sitting on the bed saying he needed to leave. My heart sank and I thought, this was how it would always be. If I ever had someone I was even slightly interested in, Richard would come around and scare them away. The Musician assured me he wasn't scared but that it may be best for him to leave.

We said our goodbyes and he left. Right away, he texted me asking what color and model of car my ex drove. When I told him, he let me know that he was being followed by a car that matched that description. He was able to lose him and then told me he'd call me when he was home safe.

Within fifteen minutes, there was a loud banging on my door. It was my ex. I contemplated what I should do and then decided to confront him. He talked me into still being my ride to the party even with the bad feeling I had in my stomach. It was obvious there was still a part of me that wasn't listening to my own gut when it came to him. Sometimes change is a forward and backward motion, even when we think we have it figured out. It didn't take long for the yelling and accusing to start. He threatened to leave me on the side of the road. This time I was angry at myself for not sticking to my own gut. I knew how this guy operated and should have never accepted a ride from him in the first place. He was very volatile and when he saw I may be moving on, he was even worse. When we got to a stop light, I got out of the car and started walking. I knew I was close to where my friends were and if I could just get to them, I'd be safe. He let me walk for a bit, then came and got me, saying he was calm and would drive me the rest of the way. I accepted, promising myself I'd never put myself in this kind of situation where he'd have any semblance of control over me ever again.

A few days later, Richard called me saying he was so depressed he was going to kill himself. He wanted to move back in so I could take care of him after an injury he'd had. There was no way in hell I was letting him into my house ever again! He owned a gun, so I called the police and let them know he had threatened suicide and warned them he had a weapon. They picked him up, and he spent a few days at the hospital. Richard never tried to pull that card on me ever again. I knew one thing for sure: I wasn't going to let him manipulate me anymore, but I was also going to take any threats of suicide very seriously.

I continued to keep my focus on myself and my happiness, staying away from anything and anyone that brought that happiness down. I started to work more on my business and became Reiki 2 certified. Although I knew I'd met a great guy, I was apprehensive because every time I'd met someone in the past, it ended up being toxic. I kept seeing both The Hunter and The Musician, being VERY honest and upfront to both of them. My number one goal was to stay true to myself and not let anyone get in the way of my happy life!

Following only what brings you happiness really changes you. It brings you away from what people call "drama" and takes you to a place where that has a hard time existing. As soon as something feels bad, it becomes much easier to walk away from it. Before, I would've held on for dear life. Even when my ex husband went off on The Hunter in public, I didn't dwell there. If he wasn't going to want to spend time with me because of my ex, it was his decision and I'd respect it, but I wouldn't beg to be a part of anyone's life, nor would I put my wants and needs to the side for someone else.

As time went on, The Hunter became more and more pushy to be in a one-on-one relationship. The

Musician, on the other hand, told me he wouldn't push me into anything I wasn't ready for. He reassured me he wanted to be exclusive but would wait for me to be ready. He only asked that if I knew I didn't want to be with him, I'd be honest and let him know my feelings. This started to make The Hunter less appealing and The Musician more appealing. I started to question what I wanted with either of them. As a vegetarian, could I see myself being with someone who took pleasure in taking the life of other creatures? Could I allow a possible future child to be taught that it was acceptable to do that? The answers were no. The reality was, he was a wonderful man... for someone else. Although the sex was great, sex wasn't going to hold a relationship together for a lifetime, and our values were too different. It was a bit of a relief to really understand that. I think I'd been relying on hormones in most of my past relationships instead of thinking long term. It wasn't easy, but I broke it off with him.

You would assume this would make it easier to make a decision about The Musician. He wasn't pushy, we had so much chemistry, and so many things in common. So what did I start to think about? Breaking it off. In fact, on three separate occasions, I'd decided that being in a relationship wasn't really what I wanted at all. I enjoyed my freedom too much to be "tied down" to anyone. Since he was such a wonderful man, I should probably release him so he could make some other woman happy. For me, every other relationship had been about "losing my freedom" and taking something away from me. I was scared. However, each time I'd make the decision to break it off, he'd look at me with his brilliantly shiny blue eyes, so filled with love, and I'd feel this overwhelming sense of loss. I felt like I'd be missing out on something amazing if I didn't give him a chance. I'd joke with him, saying that he wouldn't be good at playing poker because he was constantly showing me his hand and asking if it was good.

For the New Year, I decided to let him know I wanted to be exclusive. It looked like he'd won the lottery; he even reminded me that he wasn't pressuring me to be exclusive if I wasn't ready. I reassured him that I was, and wanted to be more serious about giving him a chance.

Things were going really well until the first good guy I'd ever dated, Montana, got in touch with me. This was my "guy that got away" in a lot of ways. This threw me for a loop. Here I was with a wonderful man, but there definitely was some unfinished business with Montana. I wasn't going to allow anyone to keep me from "missing out" so I decided to meet up with him for dinner. We had a wonderful time! He was still as handsome as ever, a huge go-getter, and such a gentleman. He told me how he'd tried to date but hadn't met any other women like me. He said he may have made a mistake when he broke things off, admitting it was one of the hardest decisions he'd ever made. He didn't have fun with anyone the way he had with me. Montana left, and I felt very confused. Here were two examples of very different good men. I again asked myself if I should end the relationship with The Musician.

I figured I'd do things slightly differently. I'd ask Montana what he wanted to do and go from there. It ended up that he still wasn't sure. He was in a place emotionally that I'd been in about two years prior, and I was no longer willing to compromise myself and wait for someone to figure things out. I wasn't willing to put all of my emotions and effort into someone that wasn't equally as excited to be with me. It was the closure I needed. I would never have to wonder if he really was the one that got away; I knew he just wasn't the guy for me.

Once I made that decision, I let The Musician know that I had seen Montana. I was ready for him to get angry or jealous but the exact opposite happened. He asked me how I felt and if I'd gotten the closure I needed. What a different experience it was to not feel defensive! Being totally and completely honest with the person I was dating was such a relief! I didn't have to be scared or worried that he was going to be angry at me, which made it so much easier to be totally upfront and honest. All of this showed me one important piece of him. He'd become my friend above anything else and as a friend, he was willing to put my needs and wants above his own if it meant I was happy. He showed me who he was without trying to control or manipulate me. The Musician wanted to support me in becoming the best version of myself, without any ulterior motives. That's actually the definition of love: to want someone to be happy even if that means it's not with you. No need to control anyone!

We quickly became closer and closer as the walls started to come down. We spoke of getting married and having children, and I told him my fears of marriage. I wasn't sure if I could get married again because of how my ex had changed after we got married. He said he understood and reminded me that he'd be honored to share life's journey with me no matter how that was.

After a time when I was late for my period, the talk of having a child together came up. I had dreams that a little soul wanted to be our child. I hadn't imagined having a child with any of the other men that I'd been with. For the first time in my life, I got excited about the idea of this man being the father of my child, of him being the one to teach a child to be a good human being. As worried as I was about being married, the thought of having a child together became exciting! I warned him that I had medical issues that may keep me from having a child, so it might not actually happen. He reassured me he was ready for whatever "the universe" was going to give to us. We decided to see what happened. Six weeks later we found out I was pregnant during a doctor's visit! Through all the years of thinking I may not be able to have children and all of the bad things I'd dealt with, I was finally in a place where the word "pregnancy" filled me with so much love and excitement. Being able to share the experience with this man crumbled away the fear of marriage and commitment. We were married six weeks later, surrounded by our family and closest friends in a small ceremony on the beach by my parents' house, officiated by my best friend. The day (and night!) was everything I hoped it could be. It was the dream wedding I deserved after finding a man that was a true partner and best friend.

Stephanie McPhail

**Marrying my best friend, the happiest day of my life-next to the
birth of my son!**

Stephanie and David-More than I ever could have imagined!

It was a long and difficult journey. There are moments where it feels like the years of bad relationships happened to someone else. But they didn't. I'm stronger and more appreciative of what I have now because of those lessons I had to endure. I can think back to when I was scared and embarrassed to leave and how difficult it was. I tear up thinking that all of this amazing life I live now wouldn't be possible had I not made those decisions and did the work on myself I had to do. To think that this reality may not have happened hurts my heart. What hurts more is knowing how many people out there are still stuck living a life they're not happy with, while missing out on the amazing life that's waiting for them. I know the mountain may seem insurmountable at times, like it's just too hard, you're too old, too poor, too dependent, have kids, etc. If it was easy to make hard decisions, then everyone would be living the life they deserve.

But it's not always easy. Sometimes leaving is one of the hardest decisions you can make. It's not your fault that anyone is treating you badly, but it is up to you to remind yourself that you don't have to stay in that story. You can start creating a new life based on what you think may only be a dream. It's your soul "tugging" you, reminding you that the life you want is not only possible, but it's actually calling for you! Remember: you are way stronger than you realize!

"Being Loved Shouldn't Hurt"

Honeymoon in Costa Rica

Family trip to France where we lived for a month!

"Being Loved Shouldn't Hurt"

Château de Versailles, France

Sacre Coeur, France

Chapter 2
Catie's Story

With all the shit I've allowed myself to be put through from men, one would have thought that I was raised by abusive and horrible people. But in reality, I was raised by loving parents. My mother passed away when I was young and my father quickly remarried and left me to my own devices when it came to men. I was never shown how to date or even how to act.

Men became my obsession to fill the void of my mother dying and my father forgetting about his teenage daughter. I wanted a man to love me, to make me feel whole. I tried so hard to date, and I guess my desperation was really what led me down this treacherous path.

I was in my first abusive relationship when I was 22 years old. We were too young to live together, but I was so desperate for love that I put up with it. He was overweight and insecure. He was a typical tough guy, Italian-American. He had a hot temper and would fly off the handle easily. He was always accusing me of cheating or talking to other guys. Little by little, the fantasy that I held so dear to my heart started to vanish. I made more money than him, and he always held it over my head. Every morning, he'd tell me how fat and ugly I was and how no other man would love me. I started to despise him, but I was trapped. We shared money, insurance, everything! It was a "mini-marriage" that never got better. It left me broken. The worst part was when I went to my dad, begging him to let me live with him and away from this monster, and he said no. He said no to his own child. He did pay for me to get another apartment, but it was heartbreaking.

The funniest part about this relationship is that we were only together for nine months and clearly, it went south quickly. I'd given up. I saw my life as being married to this abusive guy with children and being miserable. I was so desperate for love that I couldn't imagine leaving him. I started to believe him when he told me all those awful things he thought of me.

One time, we got in a huge fight and he threw me into the closet door; another time he threw a remote control at me. I never knew what mood he would be in and I started to look forward to going grocery shopping without him, or doing laundry without him. I just wanted to get away from him!

One night, I was lying down and I was just so depressed and miserable. Can you imagine thinking you're so unlovable and ugly that not one guy will ever love you except for the loser that you're with at that time? I was a suicidal mess. As I laid there, I heard my mother's voice loud and clear! "Get up, out of this bed! I did not raise you to end up with this guy! You have so much more to do in your life. You are my daughter and you are strong. LEAVE." With that, I got up and I told him I was leaving. I started the process and got myself together.

I broke up with him. He was stunned. This arrogant piece of shit never thought that I'd leave him. The day I packed up the last of my things, he asked me to marry him. I laughed in his face. I told him no way! He told me how he loved me, blah blah blah. To this day, he still chases me. I'm the one who got away, but let me tell you, I'm so happy I went through that. It made me stronger and also wiser.

Years later, the guy I started to date right after this one broke up with me. We had a volatile relationship because he was a drug addict. He was abusive as well but in a different way. He was controlling and made me lose weight.

The next person I was with started showing severe signs of being abusive, we only dated 2 months. He was short and wouldn't "allow" me to wear heels taller than him. I never listened to him. Anyways, one night he and I got in a huge fight and he threw a bunch of different things at me. He then picked me up and threw me! It was insane and really scary. I wanted to leave and he didn't let me. I decided to appease him just to get him to stop. So I laid down with him and pretended everything was okay. As we were in the middle of this crazy fight, it dawned on me - because of my previous abusive relationships, I was more aware of the signs and these were HUGE red flags.

The next morning when I woke up, he looked at me and said good morning, like nothing had ever happened!! I got up and told him to fuck off and RAN away. I'd already packed the night before while he was sleeping and I peeled out of his driveway as he chased me in his bare feet down the road. He called me 60 times that day and I refused to answer. Finally, I answered and told him to never contact me again; that we were done. I changed my number but because he was a private investigator, he found out my new number and started to contact me. I threatened him with a restraining order. Since he was trying to become a cop, he backed off.

Trying to pick up the pieces of my shattered world, I tried online dating. He kept finding me and I had to block him and threaten him with a restraining order or I'd call his precinct. He always told me how he fell in love with me. Bullshit! He, along with the rest, just wanted control.

Fast forward seven years and finally, I've found my guy. It took going through a goddamned war zone before I met him, but he's here. I was single for five years before I met him and it was a great time. I dated some awesome and not so awesome guys. Some of the guys I met, I'm still friends with! I was so desperate for love I put up with so much crap that I never deserved. I used to be envious of my friends who were married with kids, but they're all divorced now. I'm so glad I never got married and I never had kids. I was waiting for the right man, and I finally met him. He too has never been married and never had kids, which was perfect since I refused to date a man with children.

I truly believe that you have to work on yourself and take care of yourself first. As I stated, I was single for five years and after dating duds, I decided to go to grad school and not worry about dating. My friend, who was recently divorced asked me to be wingman on her first online date. Her date brought his wingman and us "wingmen" clicked and are now planning on getting married next year. We weren't set up and neither of us was looking to date. He'd just had a series of terrible relationships and I was just going to focus on school and worry about dating after I graduated.

The greatest part of this whole story is when I met my now boyfriend, I was so focused on myself and not even trying to date, that when he asked me out I said no. He asked me out two more times and I finally said yes. He's very handsome, but I just didn't want to date anyone! After our first date, I was still nervous. We hung out every day after that, and it's been a fairy tale since! Every day I look at this man and am so happy to have finally found my future husband. I had to go through all of that crap, so when I found a great man, I knew it right away. We both have gone through horrible relationships so we both feel lucky to have one another.

Chapter 3
Michelle's Story

My childhood was messed up because my parents were in an unhealthy marriage. My dad was abusive, a cheater, a liar, and an all-around bad person, so I didn't have a very good role model. I developed a lot of issues with men because of that. When I was a teenager, I sought out attention from men. My mom worked a lot and was working three jobs to try and take care of us. My parents had divorced when I was ten years old, so my mom had to take care of us on her own.

My father didn't keep up with child support; he was consistent in not being reliable. I was court ordered to go and visit him every other weekend, even when I didn't want to, or he didn't make any payments. I had to witness the unhealthiness and neglect with his new family too. There was a lot of fighting between them. I saw my father be physically abusive to both my mother and my stepmother.

There's one altercation that stands out because it was my first memory of violence. I blacked out the details of what happened, but I had Post-Traumatic Stress Disorder (PTSD) from it until I was 30. I'd hear any noise in the night, and it would make me scared and jumpy, which was a major turning point for me. I do remember there were hitting and punching. My dad was drunk. Things always happened when my father was drunk.

I had an older sister, and I tried to connect with her but she just pushed me away. She doesn't remember it well, but she was going through her own issues, not coping with what was happening at home. She has never fully dealt with our childhood.

Living at home was stressful. My mother tried to get me into therapy after I started acting out. She'd gotten remarried and didn't want to be bothered with me. She moved away with her new husband and wanted me to come with them. I didn't want to, so I went and lived with my grandparents. I was acting out by hanging out with gang members, running away, not coming home for days at a time at the age of 14, and cutting school. I dropped out of high school because I found out I could drop out at 16. As soon as I realized that was an option, I did it. I was already so behind, but I did eventually get my GED.

I had a boyfriend all through high school who was jealous and controlling. If I didn't give him the attention he wanted, he would mess with me by cheating on me and lying to me. So, I got back at him by cheating on him, too. He already assumed I was cheating if he couldn't find me. He would go look for me and drag me out from wherever I was. When I was 18, he called me up one day and gave me a hard time. I'd had enough and just decided to end the relationship. He was freaking out, begging me to be with him. For the next two years, he would call me, weeping and begging me to come back.

I took about two years in between relationships; it probably should have been longer. In hindsight, I realize I hadn't fully gotten the help I needed to know who I was and what I wanted in life. Had I taken more time, I probably wouldn't have started another unhealthy relationship.

I went to college for a little while but dropped out, because I met a guy and got pregnant. I wasn't planning on staying with him. We'd been together for about six months when we found out I was pregnant. I ended up staying with him for three years.

This relationship got bad very quickly, pretty much immediately. We would yell and scream and throw things at each other. We got evicted from multiple apartments. He'd cheat on me. I had a baby so I'd be home by myself with the baby, and he'd be off doing whatever he wanted for days at a time. He wouldn't pay the bills. Since I was staying home with the baby, I had no money to pay the bills. As I was going through that, I really felt miserable. Why did I stay? I felt like I had no choice. I didn't know what to do and I'd lost all control. He made me feel insecure, telling me nobody liked me or wanted to hang out with me.

I had originally started to date him because he was a "sweet talker". He had just gotten out of prison but had not told me that. He lied to me, saying he had been in Hawaii. I knew his whole family, so I felt safe with him. He had spent three years in prison for attempted murder. It took a couple of months for me to find out, but by then it was the excited "honeymoon" period. I thought it was no big deal, and we could deal with it and accept everything.

He separated me from my friends and family. He told me lies about them. They'd tell me he was trying to cheat on me but then he'd turn it around, saying they were the ones trying to come on to him. He would say they were lying and just trying to get us to break up. I felt further isolated, with just my baby. It was really rough. He was very manipulative. If he became physically violent, I'd give it right back. If he threw things, I threw things back. The police were called many times.

The first time things got really bad, I was pregnant and I found out he was cheating on me. I'd been staying at my dad's house, and he was staying at his dad's house because we had been evicted again. I went over to confront him. His dad was telling me to leave him alone and I told him I was pregnant and asked if he was kidding me. He came outside, screamed at me, threw me down, and pinned me to the ground. Still, I stayed with him; it continued to be an extremely unhealthy relationship and I stayed.

For my 21st birthday, I was really excited to be able to go out and be an adult. My grandmother was watching our son. We went out to a restaurant, had a drink, and then we were going to a club. He didn't want to go and said he was going to his friend's party instead. I didn't want to go to the party because it was my birthday; I was excited to be able to go out. When I got back from the club, he wasn't back and he was supposed to pick up my son. So, I went to get my son and brought him back home. One of my friends who was at the party called to tell me that my boyfriend was still at the party, having sex with another woman. We didn't have cell phones back then.

I tried to page him. I couldn't get in touch with him. I was so angry, I changed the locks on the apartment door. I got evicted from that apartment because he kept trying to get in, causing a scene by banging on doors and screaming. I had no place to go and no money. I moved, but then I let him come back. I was really scared. It would be good for a little while, and then it would get bad. It was a cycle that kept repeating.

"Being Loved Shouldn't Hurt"

Eventually, I got an excellent job. The bosses I worked for were nice and had a house they let us rent. It was a lot of money for the two of us, so we let friends move in. I quickly found out he was cheating on me again, this time with a stripper. So, I went with a friend to a party to blow off steam. He found out where I was, came to the party with a gun, hit me in the head, and cracked my skull open. He started yelling, accusing me of cheating with one of the guys at the party. I hadn't been doing anything at all.

There was another guy there with a gun and the whole situation was getting scary so I jumped out of a second story window to escape. When I got out, I realized he'd slashed all the tires on my car. So, I couldn't get away. When I finally made it back to my house, the entire house was trashed. All of my belongings were ruined. Special items from my grandmother were destroyed or missing.

That night was terrifying. It was an eye opener. I moved three thousand miles away with my son to get away from him. I didn't think he'd be able to find me, but he did. I knew I wasn't going to be with him anymore. When he came to find me in my new place, thousands of miles away from him, he wanted to reconcile. He promised he'd never behaved that way again and begged me to stay with him, "We'll start over. Now that we're in a new place, we can start over and it won't be like that anymore." But of course, it still was. My switch was turned off and I wasn't dealing with it anymore. Even though he had come all the way out and wanted to reconcile, I took my son and went to a shelter so that he wouldn't find us. When he finally left the area, I left the shelter and moved into my parents' house. I knew he didn't know where they lived. I didn't want him to be able to find me again.

I was 24 years old, and my son and I lived with my mom and stepfather for the next two and a half years. During this time, I dated a little bit, but I wasn't looking for anything serious. Concentrating on myself and my son was my top priority. I went back to school and started to pay off the huge debt that I'd accumulated with my ex. I got myself into a better place. I met my husband during that time. When we first met, I told him I didn't want to be in a relationship and wanted to be on my own. I'd moved out of my parents' house and had gotten my own place. I had a good job and was no longer in debt. I was in school, but I slowly let him into my life. We are now celebrating our 14th wedding anniversary!

I would suggest to anyone that's been through a rough relationship to take that time. I see too many people going right from one relationship to another and end up continuing with the unhealthy cycle. I know that my older sister is 45 and still doing that. She hasn't learned the lessons she needs to learn yet. Getting strong on your own two feet is really what changes everything.

My husband was so different from anyone else I'd ever met or dated. He was open and honest; he didn't "sweet talk", he just said what he meant. Everything he said was genuine. I'd met guys like that in the past, but I had thought they were weird. I didn't understand their mindset. He told me that every girl he met, he looked at them with the thought that he was getting to know them with the possibility of it ending up in marriage. I'd never considered that with anyone I'd ever dated. I just lived in the moment all the time. So, I wanted to learn more and see how that worked.

No matter what relationship I was in, I never thought even for a second that marriage was for me. I was never one of those girls who planned out my wedding day. As a kid, I wasn't even sure I wanted to have children at all. He was much more focused. He always knew he wanted to get married and have kids and was looking for his life partner to share that with. He came out of the womb wanting to be a good husband and a good dad. Those were the qualities that I really loved about him. He comes from a very good family, and everyone gets along well. When we got married, I was almost 28 and he was 24. We have one child together and of course, I have my son from my previous relationship. It's been a wonderful fourteen years and I'm still so grateful and so in love with him.

111

Stephanie McPhail

If I could talk to my younger self, I'd tell her that she doesn't need attention from guys to be happy. Take time to learn who you are before you devote yourself to a relationship. Learn what your passions are, especially when you're young. We often forget to focus on ourselves and focus on making someone else happy and doing what they want. We don't need to please anyone; put yourself and your needs first. Use birth control! I don't regret having my son, but it did change my path. It's so hard to tell anyone who has had a bad childhood anything because they're so fueled by emotions. It's difficult to listen to wisdom but having a mentor, someone who is in a good place, to look up to is important. Find someone to emulate; look up to that person. I didn't have that at all. I see other people that had that one person and it was so helpful to them. I didn't have that in my parents, my relationships, my sister, nor anyone else. If I could have had one person to help me through, maybe things would have been different for me. Literally, everyone who interacted with me took me down bad roads.

I know if I had stayed with my ex, I would've missed out on the opportunity to have a really healthy and supportive relationship. My kids would've missed out on having a great role model and father. I would've probably ended up being a drug addict in order to cope with how bad I felt and suppress my feelings of extreme sadness. I wouldn't be successful, and I'd still be in debt. I wouldn't have gotten an education. I was able to get a degree, buy a house, and experience all of those things because of that decision to change my life and leave. My number one motivation was to not have my son behave that way. I didn't want my son to see that as a role model. I would've missed out on the genuine love and care that I get to share with my husband.

I'd never known what it was like to see or experience love like this so I wasn't really sure it was possible for me. I saw my grandparents happily married; I just didn't see it as a possibility for me. I hoped that maybe there was a great guy out there, but that's not why I left. I didn't even care about a relationship - I just couldn't live like that anymore. I left just with the hope that I wouldn't put my son through what I'd been through. Protecting him was of utmost importance.

I'd like to be able to help more people so they don't have to go through all of this. My best words to leave you with are "Just like when escaping a fire: once out, stay out."

Chapter 4
Jordan's Story

I don't know if you know anything about being brought up Born Again Christian, but my experience was very interesting, to say the least. I wasn't allowed to dress up and go trick-or-treating, do anything that involved dressing up or watch certain television shows. These things were associated with the devil and it was seen as a sin.

I was the third child out of four children and we were all very close. In my childhood, my parents were always fighting, and both of them were suffering from different types of substance abuse issues. They finally got divorced when I was nine. The courts decided that my mother would get custody with us. After the divorce, she leaned more and more on the alcohol and that meant my siblings and I mostly raised ourselves. Things were better than when my parents were together and fought all the time, but it was still far from a picture perfect upbringing. I'm happy to say that my mother got sober, but it wasn't until I was about seventeen years old, so learning how to take care of myself was a task I had to navigate on my own.

My dad, on the other hand, didn't drink alcohol but used cocaine on occasion. But what really ended up being his demise was Oxycontin and then heroin. Those were his drugs of choice. Of course looking back, he was a diabetic who had really poor eating habits. I would say sugar was also his drug of choice. All of those things combined ended up being what killed him.

It's strange because even with all of the dysfunction in my family, I knew that I was loved. I got beaten as a child when I did something wrong, but I wasn't overly upset by that, I feel like it was part of the culture of raising children at the time. My father was a very complex and abusive man. There was a lot of fear-based threats in the household because of that. That was, until I was nine when my mom finally decided she had enough and left. Then his his thing became manipulating us with money. He would threaten us with needing to behave in ways that he approved of in order for him to send my mom any money for us.

When I was thirteen, my older brother showed me the first couple of chords of a song on my guitar that only had two strings. I was obsessed immediately. From then on, music was my outlet. Through all of the fucked up stuff going on at home, it was my "constant", and since my family had a lot of painters and musicians they were very supportive of my creativity. Between music, yoga and connecting with friends, those things were my saving grace and got me through my worst years. To this day, I know that if I am not using my outlets, then something is wrong and I need to reconnect with myself. This is so important for my mental health; it is my "medicine".

Stephanie McPhail

When I was 21, I had my first spiritual awakening. Growing up in a very Christian household, I needed my relationship with my spirituality to be repaired. Especially because of my sexuality (I identified as a lesbian at the time), the lies of the church led me to believe that I was doomed to go to hell. I started reconnecting with that part of myself and did 100 hours of my first yoga teacher training, I discovered how much I loved to use my body to work through my emotions. I also discovered the universe of truth and love inside myself. Soon after I started the training, I got burnt out. It was "too soon" for me. I wasn't ready for that amount of change yet, but I had not given up. I started to read spiritual texts from all different philosophies of thought and became more aware and connected with my spirituality.

The strange thing about dysfunctional families is that we keep trying to help each other no matter what effect it has on us. I think it has a lot to do with the statements in the Bible such as "Honor thy mother and thy father". I moved in with my dad for a bit after high school. Part of me thought I would be able to help him with his lifestyle habits. Living in his house, I never knew who I was going to see when I stepped out of the shower; it might have been no one or it might be a "crackhead" or a heroin addict. He was selling prescription pills as his main source of income and had gotten my older brother to start selling them as well. I seemed to care more about his health than he did and it was killing me. At 19 I moved out of his house, and at the age of 23, I stopped all communication with him. I never even read the letters he had written to me. Making that decision was a huge turning point for me as far as my self-worth was concerned. Everything about my relationship with my father was toxic and had I continued it, nothing good would have come, and I wouldn't have been able to make room for the good in my life. I left in anger, but the anger served a purpose, it propelled me to make a choice that I needed to make.

Two years later, he died, and I was never able to reconcile with him. This ate me up inside for a while. I had a very hard time forgiving myself for not speaking to him before he died. What made matters worse was that fifty-two days after my father passed away, my older brother passed away as well. I was grieving and that is where I stayed for a long time. When you are going through major grief and are still functioning in an unhealthy way, you attract that. This was no different for me. I got married less than a year after my brother and father died, and consequently, my marriage was a reflection of my unhealthiness.

I had known for a long time that I wanted to transition to become a man. After I lost my father and brother and got married, I decided that I needed to take care of myself and become more comfortable with who I was. I worked four different jobs, took out a small medical loan and paid for my top surgery. After two years of being unhappy, my wife and I decided to part ways and get a divorce. The divorce was the icing on the cake for me. This shovelled me into a dark depression.

After the divorce, I started to work more towards self- improvement. I'm not going to lie, I was sleeping around a bit, but it was part of what I needed at the time. I knew that I was depressed and knew that the best way to get out of the slump I was in was to make a major change. I had heard a friend of mine tell me about going to India to get certified as a yoga teacher. and I knew that I needed to get out of the environment I was in. I decided I was going to go to India to learn yoga, why the fuck not? I literally had nothing to lose at that point in my life. I went and got my passport and visa, found a school, and bought my plane ticket. There was no going back after that.

Before going to India, I had gotten myself into a much better place. I had become my own best friend, started to really take care of my health and even got acupuncture and massage treatments a few times a month. When I went to India, I told myself I was just going to focus on myself and my practice and I wasn't going to seek out any type of romantic relationship with anyone. I wanted to focus on the yoga journey that was before me, and obviously the universe had other plans for me.

In India, it was my first time as a single man! I was a woman, then I was married, then I transitioned into a man, and then I was divorced. I was able to be myself in all forms. I was starting to connect with myself in ways I never was able to before, which was very freeing. No matter who you are, after major traumatic events, it's hard to bounce back. It's also hard to find people that are working towards constantly evolving spiritually and intellectually. When you are on a path of growth, the road can be lonely at times. There are many people that say they want change, but there is no action involved. I have found that making real change allows us to find our truth and can be the most rewarding experience. It also means that we lose friends along the way, but meet new people who are on the same path.

Once in India, I began to feel a connection that I had never experienced before. The school wasn't sure what to do with me because I was doing the training mostly on my own. For part of my 300 hours of training, they sent me to a meditation center for what was supposed to be 14 days. When I got there, I was overwhelmed with how beautiful it was, but also how something didn't feel "right". It was an Osho meditation center and felt a bit like a cult. For those who don't know, Osho has a huge following but, but he is also dead. Once someone dies I have noticed the ideas may live on but they are no longer being implemented by the person who had the vision so things can get twisted a bit. To me, this place had made the Yoga/Spiritual journey into a money situation and had lost integrity with what he would have done. One of the meditations they even made you yell out his name! That really turned me off.

For two days, I couldn't sleep - things were "off". I have learned to trust my intuition on these things. I felt like shit, it was the first time I felt really bad in India. I searched my soul as to why I was upset and it came down to instinct. I was getting bad vibes from the whole place. I had an intuition - I felt like I was running late for something and that I had to be somewhere else. I felt like I had to leave. I left early and went back to my training center. When I got back to my school, I saw this beautiful blonde woman. She was on a silent day and couldn't talk, but we made eye contact. The first time we saw each other was at the auspicious fire ceremony to open up her classes during yoga teacher training month. It was one of those moments that you never forget. The moment when my timeline changed, love at first sight, and a recognition of a great love from a past life. I was chosen to be her teacher and when she was done with her silent day we started talking we didn't stop. I was her teacher, so although there was definitely a connection while we got to know each other on a purely friendship level. Time would fly by while we talked. After a month of spending every free moment together, we decided to break it off with our other relationships. In those spaces, you are so sensitive and fragile that you have to keep your head on straight and watch out for anyone who is not coming from a loving place. So, before her, I had my guard up. A lot of things happen very quickly in India, and those circumstances, things are understood on a more spiritual level.

Unlike any other relationship I have ever experienced, we just "clicked". On her graduation, we "sealed the deal" if you will. After all those months of getting to know each other, we finally made the relationship into a physical one. The next day, we hiked the Himalayas and then started to make plans for our next steps. I had to move out of my place a few days later, so we decided to get a place together for the remainder of our time in India. I was in India for a total of seven months. Once it was time to leave, we decided we didn't want to leave each other's side. We made plans to move back to her home country of Norway, but, since then, we also lived in America, Peru are now back in Norway. She challenges me in a way that no one else ever has. She doesn't let me fall into pity and feeling bad for myself. She is the epitome of what unconditional love is.

Maria is her name. She is sober and is talking the talk and walking the walk. She changes with me and is always evolving. I am so lucky! I thank God every day for her and feel so fortunate to have her in my life. It's so special to find someone to walk the path with you, but to also be be non- controlling or possessive. These were all great qualities that I had given up on until Maria came into my life. I feel that my consistent practice of yoga really brought change in my life on so many different levels and helped bring me to the love of my life.

It's very interesting. Now that I have been on this journey I look back and think "who the hell was that?" Now I would never let anyone treat my friends or myself as badly as I had allowed others to treat me for so many years. If i had not made the changes I did I would still be in hell. In fact, I may no longer even be alive. I discovered with a lot of work on myself that hell is on earth and we create it in our own lives. It is always a choice. To give up your power and put it in someone else's hands is a mistake - you need to take back your power, or else you will just continue to put that power into someone else's hands.

When love hurts so much, and you are so used to that hurt being love, it's hard to realize that it doesn't have to stay that way. Once you start to turn that around, actual healthy love can feel so foreign. Real love can feel wrong! You may realize that you don't want to be in a toxic relationship that makes you nervous and doesn't allow you to grow, but when you try to change it, you may actually feel you deserve the bad treatment or that you can't experience real love. People stick with the familiar because it's what they are used to. My advice for anyone looking for major change is to go with the unfamiliar and allow yourself to feel that discomfort and "relearn" what is okay and not okay for you, without anyone else's control. The more you try to experience the "unfamiliar", the more comfortable you will become. Once you have left something toxic, don't allow yourself to second guess yourself. When you first leave it, will be really difficult and you may even think you made a mistake because you are hurting so much. Don't go back. The pain will ease, you will get stronger, and as you grow you will even get to a point where you will look back and ask yourself why you stayed as long as you did. Don't get angry at yourself and let go of the guilt. The most important thing to remember is that you got out and now have the possibility to fall back in love with yourself by treating yourself VERY VERY well. The next time someone comes to sweep you off your feet, they had better be ready to treat you as well as you treat yourself.

The worst thing you can do is to stay. There are so many people that I know that were in shitty relationships, and when I speak to them again they are back in the bad relationships. Nothing changed but they go back anyway because it's what they know. You will not change anyone and the only person you need to work on is yourself. Complaining about being in a bad relationship and looking for sympathy will not help. Decide to make a change and move forward with your life. You need to go through your own shit before things can get better. Looking for someone else to come and save you and make things better is a sure way of making the same mistakes all over again. You need to not only cut ties in your relationship with your significant other, but also cut ties with your old "self patterns" for change to be possible.

I will leave you with this phrase I heard from a random stranger that really resonated with me. He said, "you can lie to yourself, lie to your wife, lie to your pastor and lie to your friends, but you can't lie to your body." If you are noticing yourself using negative ways to deal with your life and feel sad more often than not, it's your body telling you something. Start listening.

Jordan and Maria were officially married under man's law in Oslo, Norway on February 16, 2018. Jordan continues to teach yoga wherever he goes and he hopes to bring this knowledge to the LGBTQIA communities across the world. In addition to teaching, Jordan is a Reiki practitioner, musician, and is working on a documentary titled "Their Hope : An Untold

"Being Loved Shouldn't Hurt"

Transgender Narrative" For more information about Jordan or how to reach him you can visit

www.color-outside-the-lines.org or www.theirhopedocumentary.com

Jordan and Maria in India

Stephanie McPhail

Jordan and Maria in Oslo, Norway

"Being Loved Shouldn't Hurt"

Part Two

Chapter 5
What is Codependency?

"Codependence is the pain in adulthood that comes from being wounded as a child." **Carol Cannon**

Reading these stories, you may have had a lot of things going on in your mind. One may have been, "Wow, I can't even believe how much I can relate to this." Another feeling may have been "This is nothing like what I have experienced." Or you may even be making excuses, saying "Well he/she never hit me; I messed up too." All I can ask you is: are you happy? The big question I asked myself that started me down my new path out of unhealthy relationships was: If I were to die tomorrow, would I be happy with the life that I lead? I visualized myself living like I'd been living in 30 years from now, thought of all of the opportunities of love and life I would be missing out on, and I honestly answered. No. There had to be more to life than crying all the time. Although I'd never experienced any healthy intimate romantic relationships, I felt it was important that I figured out how to experience that. Other areas of my life were being negatively affected and I knew it was keeping me from fully living my best life.

If you're reading this book, you're probably questioning whether you are in an unhealthy relationship. If you have to ask yourself that question, then you already know the answer. Maybe you're just not ready to deal with the reality yet. So before we go on, let's talk about codependency, because chances are good that you may fit into this category. Don't worry, you are not alone; it's way more common than you may realize.

In her book *Codependent No More*, author Melody Beattie defines codependency as follows:

"A codependent person is one who has let another person's behavior affect him or her and who is obsessed with controlling that person's behavior."

The good news is, if you fall into the category of codependency, then it means you're a *survivor*. You did whatever you knew to do to cope. Sadly, holding onto these behaviors in your adult life can be detrimental to all future relationships. Let me pause for a moment here and just make sure you don't think I blame you for being treated badly. In fact, you're an amazing person to be so giving and willing to help someone you love.

So what is a dysfunctional family? A dysfunctional family can be outlined in a few different ways but for this book let's keep it simple: it's a "family that consists of one or both parents having issues that interfere with their functions as parents." This can include mental disorders, drug or alcohol addiction, some kind of sexual or physical abuse, dealing with an explosive temper, chronic illness, death of a parent at a young age, and in a lot of cases it may be more than one issue going on at the same time. The reason why kids in these types of families learn codependency is because they have had to act in the roll of a parent while they're still children and not yet ready to take on that responsibility. They have not had the chance to grow up and are already being expected to act in adult ways. In a dysfunctional family, members suffer from worry, anger, pain, or shame that's ignored, denied, or hidden away. This teaches children that this kind of behavior is acceptable; they believe love and family always include these feelings.

I think that because of my parent's marital issues and whatever my mother was going through while I was growing up, she spoke to me more like I was a friend than her daughter. I knew all too well how unhappy she was in the marriage and how angry she was with my father. I love my parents and am so grateful to them, but it wasn't easy growing up. My father had a bad temper but the positive thing was that at least we knew that $A+B=C$. There was consistency. If we didn't do a chore or whatever we were told, we'd be punished. Before 13 that definitely meant being spanked with a belt or whatever other objects were around. My mom on the other hand was not quite as simple. We never knew what was going to make her angry with us. Sometimes we could do something and it'd make her laugh and the next day we'd say or do the same thing and she'd get angry. There wasn't a lot of consistency. After a fight with my father, my mother would lock herself in the bedroom and not come out until my dad begged at the door to talk. She'd let him in and after a little while they'd both come out and we had to act like everything was OK and get back to normal. We never heard apologies from either of them, we just had to be happy it was over and pretend everything was OK. We never experienced how to reconcile in a healthy way.

Codependency can be passed down through generations as it did in my family. It is most common in families who have had to deal with a parent's substance abuse issues, death of a parent at a young age or a parent with a mental illness. Codependency keeps people from having mutually satisfying, healthy relationships and has also been known as "relationship addiction." The fear of being alone drives a lot of people who are codependent into staying in ANY relationship, even if it's toxic or abusive. These kinds of relationships are often one sided and emotionally destructive. More often than not, the codependent person is trying to help "save" their partner or parent at all costs, even if it's painful or unhealthy for their own well being. That was me. It was also true for my parents. My father had come from an abusive family where he was beaten on a regular basis and his mother was too. He had to become a protector for his little brother and mother. My mom also came from an abusive father who would beat up her mother and have affairs. She became very afraid of her father and developed a very close relationship with her mother because they were surviving together. Neither of them came from the best examples of what a healthy and happy relationship could be. I fully believe they did the best they could and that they did way better than what they were shown growing up.

You may feel you had a great example of what a healthy marriage could be and question why you got into a relationship that doesn't feel right. So then how did you fall into this pattern? No matter what your background is, a big part of codependency is self-esteem. How do you feel about yourself? Do you feel sure of yourself? Do you feel that you're deserving of real love that feels good? Do you feel that it's your right to be treated well? If the answer is no to any of those questions, you may have just figured out how you became codependent.

I often tell the story of the frog in the pot. If you were going to throw a frog in boiling water, it'd jump out. However, if you put a frog in cold water and then slowly increase the temperature until it boils, it'll stay in until it boils to death. We're the same way. If someone called you a bitch on the first date, you'd tell them to go to hell and never look back. When you come from a family where fighting and anxiety were normal for people, then your tolerance for crap is way higher.

"Being Loved Shouldn't Hurt"

If you come from a family that was quiet and happy, then your tolerance may be much lower. That doesn't mean you can't fall into a codependent relationship either way; it's just easier for the person that came from the stressful background. Think about drug addiction. If your family has a history of drug abuse, the chances are greater that you can become an addict. However, ANYONE can become an addict if the situation is right. It's the same thing with relationships.

Let's say you're in a relationship with someone who's addicted to drugs. You may feel frustrated, angry, hurt, lied to, etc. All normal feelings, right? What you do will determine the outcome. Do you tell them what you want, set up boundaries, and adhere to those boundaries? Or do you make excuses for their behavior, pick them up whenever they need a ride, and give them money? That's codependency. Even though it hurts you, and hurts them as well, you do everything in your power to "help them." Why go so out of your way for someone who wouldn't do the same for you? Not that you should do things with expectations, but if you notice it's constantly you helping out the same person and it's hurting you - that's not a healthy balanced relationship.

Being a victim is not a good place to be. It's a disempowering belief that someone else is responsible for saving us. It's not anyone else's job but your own. Just like it isn't our job to "fix" anyone else. If they're not ready to do the work they need to do, no amount of "helping" on our part is going to get them there. It's also not not very attractive to constantly "nag" people to make changes. Think of when you kept being told to do something you didn't want to do, how did you react? It doesn't matter how dysfunctional the behavior is, if it's not coming from the person then they're not going to fix it. The healthier response is to allow them to learn from their own journey while not disempowering them to make their own changes. My two long-term relationships were with people who had some major issues. The more I explained and complained and the more frustrated I became with them for not changing, the worse things got. This was a waste of my time and energy. Why? Because *they* were the ones that needed to decide on their own that they needed change. Looking back, it would have cost me less money and time had I explained my boundaries and when I saw they were not able to meet them, I should have walked away.

If, after reading all of this, you are still not sure whether or not you are codependent, talk to a therapist who can help you get to the root of the issue and help figure out how to heal and transform old unserving patterns. The word itself doesn't matter; the bigger issue is realizing that things need to change in order for you to be happy, because whatever you are doing now isn't working. Remember, it took years to get to where you are now, it's going to take some time to get you where you need to be. Get all the positive help you can get from people who are in a healthy place themselves.

The following is a list of some typical characteristics of codependency. Take out a piece of paper and make a checklist, or check them off right in your book if it's related to you. If you notice that you're checking off a lot of these statements, it's extra important to get someone to help you make changes!

- Do you always need things to be perfect and fear failure?
- Do you feel guilty setting boundaries?
- Do you feel like a victim?
- Are you sensitive to criticism?
- Do you focus on other people's wants instead of your own needs?
- Are you uncomfortable receiving attention?
- Do you feel responsible for the feelings or actions of others?
- Do you have low self-esteem or a weak sense of identity?
- Do you feel alone, abandoned, angry, sad, ashamed, or helpless?
- Do you blame others for how you feel and wait for someone to come save you?
- Do you feel empty, bored, and worthless unless you have someone to take care of or a crisis to solve?

- Do you do everything your new partner does, forgetting about your own interests? Do you find it difficult to find satisfaction in other aspects of your life?
- Do you see toxic behavior from your partner but find it difficult to admit you're in a dysfunctional relationship?
- Do you stay in unhealthy relationships, not vocalizing your needs and tolerating abuse in order to keep people loving you?
- Do you go from one bad relationship to another one?

Chapter 6
Why do people stay in codependent relationships?

"Making a big life change is pretty scary. But know what's even scarier? Regret." **Zig Ziglar**

If you are like me, you have heard over and over again, "Why did you stay? Why didn't you leave when they started treating you so badly?" People who have never experienced abuse in any form have a hard time really empathizing. So why did I stay? This is a tricky area. Most relationships start off with good times. Again, they don't call you a "bitch" on the first date! Almost all abusers follow a similar pattern: they start off overly sweet, show you attention, tell you how attractive you are, and they go out of their way to act like Prince/Princess Charming. They shower you with gifts, start talking about a future together, use the word "love" very quickly, and often want to move in together immediately. Not everyone fits into every aspect of this, but it's the same basic story each time. This is called the "honeymoon period". For anyone who had a fantasy of getting married and living happily ever after, this period is important. It gives a false sense of security. You see this person saying and doing all the right things, and you start to let your guard down. This is what they need.

I'm sure you've heard the term "Cycle of Abuse." Most abusive relationships follow this cycle: tension building, acting out, reconciling, and calm. However, when the abuser is a narcissist, the cycle can look different. Licensed Medical Health Counselor Christine Hammond shows the Narcissistic Cycle of Abuse as follows:

Feels threatened - An upsetting event occurs and the narcissist feels threatened. It could be rejection of sex, disapproval at work, embarrassment in a social setting, jealous of other's success, or feelings of abandonment, neglect, or disrespect. The abused, aware of the potential threat, becomes nervous. They know something is about to happen and begin to walk on eggshells around the narcissist. Most narcissists repeatedly get upset over the same underlying issues whether the issue is real or imagined. They also have a tendency to obsess over the threat repeatedly.

Abuses others. The narcissist engages in some sort of abusive behavior. The abuse can be physical, mental, verbal, sexual, financial, spiritual, or emotional. The abuse is customized to intimidate the abused in an area of weakness, especially if that area is one of strength for the narcissist. Sometimes a combination of two types of abuse is used. For instance, a narcissist may begin with verbal belittling to wear out the abused. This is followed by projection of their lying about an event onto the abused. Finally tired of the assault, the abused defensively fights back.

Becomes the victim. This is when the "switchback" occurs. The narcissist uses the abused behavior as further evidence that they are the ones being abused. The narcissist believes their own twisted victimization (by bringing up past defensive behaviors that the abused has done) as if the abused initiated the abuse. Because the abused has feelings of remorse and guilt, they accept this warped perception and try to rescue the narcissist. This might include giving into what the narcissist wants, accepting unnecessary responsibility, placating the narcissist to keep the peace, and agreeing to the narcissistic lies.

Feels empowered. Once the abused have given in or given up, the narcissist feels empowered. This is all the justification the narcissist needs to demonstrate their rightness or superiority. The abused has unknowingly fed the narcissistic ego and only to make it stronger and bolder than before. But every narcissist has an Achilles heel and the power they feel now will only last till the next threat to their ego appears. (Hammond, 2015)

So why don't we leave once we realize there's a cycle of abuse? It's interesting that as a society we always ask that question first. If you were brought up in a religious household, as I was, you are trained that once you get married, you stay married and you "make it work." You don't "abandon family" when they need you. You need to be loyal and put others ahead of you. In theory this may sound good, but it's not. Those things are important, but they're not more important than your own well-being. Depending on your religious background, there may also be the ideology that the man is head of the household. In a male-dominated patriarchal society like America, it's easier to defer back to the man while taking power away from the woman. This can also go the other way around, if a woman is abusing a man he may be less likely to share what is happening out of fear of not being "manly enough." In same-sex couples the abuse is even more likely not to be reported because of lack of support in the mental healthcare field.

The other problem is that abusers start to make you question your own sanity and your role in how bad the relationship is. My ex used to use projection; he would accuse me of things he was doing. He admitted he knew how badly he was treating me and couldn't understand why I wasn't leaving him. They are good at pointing out the time you lost your temper, even if it was for good reason, which messes with your mind and makes you think you're no better than they are. When you try to explain to them, they can never actually empathize with where you're coming from, because you're just an object for them to control and manipulate.

The victim also goes into survival mode. If you have children, you're trying to protect your kids and you know they'll try to use the kids against you if you leave. I would try to placate my ex. I received calls and texts that threatened to call the police, go to my job, call every new relationship I had, have my "body disappear", or kill himself. All of those things scared me. The reality is ¾ of people that die from domestic violence situations do so after they leave the relationship. It isn't easy knowing that you can't foresee what their behavior is going to be like, or sometimes worse when you already know how it will be!

There is, so often, one step forward and two steps back when it comes to leaving or changing our own behaviors. There is often a feeling of placating the partner. It may be easier at times to be nice rather than deal with them being erratic. That meant giving in at times, especially when I was depressed and had no one to help me.

I was the one with the house; I was the one who made better money. There are a lot of people who stay because they're financially dependent on their partner, especially if they have children together. Luckily this wasn't the case for me, and it was still very difficult. I also feel that age can be an issue. I saw all of my friends getting married and was so afraid of ending up alone, I held onto the possibility of what our marriage could be if we figured out the issues. Those issues were never going to be figured out, because things won't change unless each person is committed to changing. I was speaking to a social worker who works in domestic violence situations and she said she had never seen an abuser change. Additionally, some people just don't bring out the best in each other.

Once we re "roped in" by the fairy tale, things change. Why is it we tell little girls that when a little boy is mean to her, he likes her? We become accustomed to making excuses for boys/men. This isn't to say women can't be just as bad; constantly blaming erratic behavior or a bad mood on their period is no way to go through life. From the time we are small, we read or watch fairy tales. Normally, a parent is not in the picture, and a guy comes to swoop the girl off her feet and save her from her life. The "Damsel in Distress" never saves herself, she waits for someone else to save her.

When someone has healthy boundaries, they have a healthy sense of who they are as individuals. They engage in appropriate self-care while also caring for others. The are able to tell people what they want and need, and able to enforce that. In the face of criticism, they are able to maintain a basic core of self-worth. If you have never been listened to when you set boundaries, then it's easier to feel like what you're saying isn't important. This isn't healthy.

What I have found in speaking with people who have ended toxic relationships is that both partners often felt trapped. If you talk to both people in the relationship, they may explain how hard they tried and how frustrated they were with the other person, but they stayed anyway. This is not romantic. This is a lack of education about what a healthy relationship is! Both people may feel they are doing the right thing, but it's actually toxic for both of them. Believe it or not, just because you're attracted to someone doesn't mean they are the right partner for you.

This brings us to a good question to ask yourself if you're currently still in a bad relationship. Think about living this way for the rest of your life. What will you miss out on? If you died tomorrow, would you be able to look back and say you were happy and lived the best life possible?

How do you leave in a healthy way?

I'm going to give some suggestions, but please also call your local domestic violence support group. They can give you the best information for your state and your specific situation. Here are some of the things I did:

1. Save as much money as you can.

I'd take $100 at a time and hide it in the back of my stocking drawer in case I had to grab money and run. When things got worse, I kept a bag of clothes, money, and important paperwork in my car. You may not have the ability to do this, but if possible, it's a good idea.

2. You need to be the one that leaves.

This gives you power back over your life. It's so important to make the first move. When you leave, be prepared to never see any of your things again. When I left, I left my house that I owned before him. I was at the point that he could have set the whole thing on fire and I wouldn't have cared. It was about regaining my life and my own safety. If you have pets, they may try to use their safety against you as well. Do everything in your power to bring them with you, but remember that your safety (and if you have kids, their safety) is top priority. Even if your relationship doesn't have much violence, it's still best for you to leave first. Removing yourself from whatever chaos is going on at home is better for your sanity.

3. Find a place to stay.

I was lucky enough to be able to stay at my friend's house for three months. I offered to cook for her every day to repay her. It's best to be somewhere they can't find you. If you have to go to a shelter, then go. It's temporary; this period will pass. If you don't leave, you'll keep living the nightmare forever.

4. If you have even the slightest feeling you could be in danger, go to the police. Press charges and file a restraining order.

For many of us, we have lost sight of what abuse is. Most police stations have a domestic violence advocate or local agencies that will go with you. They will help you fill out the forms properly and help jog your memory of what actual abuse is. Don't feel bad about using local agencies. They are free and they are there for you.

5. Call your phone company and make sure you have a password associated with your account.

If you cannot block them for whatever reason, then change your number. If you have children, and you need to keep in contact with your ex, then decide with your lawyer what that communication will look like and entail.

6. Go "Grey Rock".

They are going to try whatever they can to get you back. They will "sweet talk", saying all the right things. It is important to remind yourself that you've been down this road before. They will never change, no matter how hard you try to help them! You need to allow them to be who they are, away from you. After you don't respond to the sweet messages, the nasty ones will start (or vice versa). Don't read the messages or listen to the voicemails, but don't delete them. It's important to save them.

7. If you are married, especially if you have kids, get a lawyer right away.

Chances are good your ex won't play nice because they want to get back at you for ending the cycle. I know they can be expensive and that's an issue for many people. I lost a lot of money ending the bad relationships I was in, and I can tell you it was worth every penny. Do I wish I didn't have to lose all that money? Of course, but at least I was safe, I knew my rights, I wasn't legally attached to them anymore, and that's all that mattered to me.

8. Be prepared for "Gaslighting".

This is the term used to describe what happens so often at the end of the relationship. It means the other person is making up information to try to make themselves look or feel better about the breakup. The automatic response for a lot of us is to defend ourselves or go out of our way to make sure people know the truth. This is a waste of time. Allow them to say whatever they want to say. The right people will know right away what's really going on, and most of the other people will see with time. It's not your job to educate people.

If you are still in an unhealthy relationship pay close attention to the following:

Ask yourself if you feel fulfilled.

In other words, do you feel like you have an equal partner in the relationship? I so often hear people say that they're looking for their other half" in a relationship. This always makes me cringe, because if two broken people come together, it's a recipe for disaster. It may work because of its dysfunction. You should be looking for your other whole! How do you expect to have a happy relationship if you're looking for someone to fill in your gaps? If this is where you're coming from, you are capable of living on your own and fixing yourself!

Remember that "what you allow is what will continue."

I heard that phrase a lot and I was frustrated because I didn't feel like I was "allowing it." When there was a big blow up, I would tell him how it made me feel. Sometimes I would leave. The problem is, I would always go back. So every time I went back, it was a sign to him that I accepted that wrongdoing. If you allow people to treat you badly, they'll keep doing it, and it will get worse. You need to protect yourself.

Chapter 7
How do you not only heal, but become a better, stronger version of yourself?

"Lead a life of your own design, on your own terms. Not one that others or the environment have scripted for you." **Tony Robbins**

Follow your gut or instinct.

There is a reason why we have that feeling in our bodies that something is wrong: it can be used to help keep us from pain. The "fight or flight" response is that moment when we have to make a decision to stay and fight it out, or run away. For many of us who are used to dysfunction, our gut is telling us to run away, but we ignore it and stay to "fight it out." As a health teacher, I can tell you that it is not good for your body! After a while, you will start to deteriorate - you will get sick easily and in reality, shorten your life!

When I was married the first time, I would get sick all of the time. Once I left and did the work I needed to do, it was two years before I even had a sniffle. Talk about a major change! During anything bad that's ever happened in my life, I had that little voice in my head trying to help me out in the right direction. My guess is we stop listening to it because of our "training." Doing things constantly for other people means that whatever you're feeling needs to be put to the side; the voice starts to get quieter. Once you start listening to it again, it'll become stronger - as will you!

I read a book called *The Celestine Prophecy* by James Redfield.

This book helped me reconnect with my ability to read people and to follow what felt right. There's definitely a different feeling when you're doing what's best for you. I would describe it as a feeling of being pulled versus pushing up against a wall going uphill. I was able to function up the hill but it's WAY easier to just follow the path of least resistance.

Get help to heal.

If you were able to do it on your own, you would have done it already. As you heal, you can't trust your own natural instincts; you need to be open about asking for help to re-learn new patterns. You'll need someone you feel very comfortable sharing all your deepest thoughts, fears, hopes, and dreams with. If you've never spoken to a therapist before, I'd suggest starting there because there are probably deep issues you've hidden away that need help coming out. If you're already aware of those issues but want more of a guide, then a coach can be very helpful. The most important thing is to have someone you're comfortable with who asks questions, help you think, looks deeper, and doesn't let you shy away from the hard issues without giving you advice. Friends may be good to vent to, but you need a professional who knows how to help people overcome whatever is holding them back. **At my business, Mind and Body Awakenings, we look at major life change in a holistic way. We combine a variety of techniques that have proven results to get our clients further than they could've even imagined! I find that a combination of techniques can be best, along with support from healthy friends and family.**

Even before you are ready to start dating again, start making a list.

Once you get to a really healthy place, you may not want to be in any relationships anymore. Believe it or not, this is actually a very good place. The goal is not to find a relationship. The goal is to be happy. Taking time in between relationships is really important for your own growth and healing. IF you decide to share your life with someone, they should be adding to that happiness, not taking it away. So what are attributes you find attractive? Before you even start dating, think of everyone you've ever met and write down qualities you admire. Do it without thinking. Then think about your dream guy/girl. Don't downplay your dream person! Reach for the best fit for you, not a settled version. You did that already and it didn't work out.

Think of all of the things that you liked in any relationship you've had.

It could be your family, friends, or your intimate relationships. Once you get your list of have to have and definitely not, keep adding to that list. The more detail you add, the easier it is for you to know who you're looking for and the better chance you'll know when you find them! You can always add, change, or delete things as you learn more about yourself.

Start thinking about what your own thoughts are about relationships.

Do you think they're hard, unsafe, scary, frustrating? If that's the case, you may be allowing yourself to stay with unhealthy people because you're getting exactly what you're thinking. These are called limiting beliefs. They are beliefs we have that are keeping us from our greatest joy! They're also sabotaging any chance of having a healthy relationship! What are your thoughts about life in general? Does it feel like you have no control and just have to deal with the job you hate, and the relationship you feel unfulfilled in? That's another limiting belief. Change your thoughts, and you'll change your outcomes!

You also need to be very aware of the little voice in your head, the doubter, we all have it! It's that voice that says we can't achieve or that we'll fail. Instead of letting that voice keep you from being your best, use it as a tool. Take out a piece of paper and write out all the things you're feeling you won't succeed at and why. Once you do that, you have a great place to start working! These are the obstacles you must overcome! There's always a way to overcome them if you put your mind to it, figure out what they are, and get help when needed. Don't get trapped as a victim when you have the power to save yourself with the right tools!

Everyone is going to have their videos, podcasts, and books that work the best for their personal story.

I needed a bit of reconnection with the rest of the world. If you're looking for some good philosophers to follow, I'd suggest starting with Alan Watts. When I was depressed and laying in my bed not able to move, I'd watch his videos. They were inspiring and helped me to look at the world in a different way than what I was used to. Honorable mentions would also be Graham Hancock and Terence McKenna (although he could go on tangents at times). None of these really have to do with unhealthy relationships; they're just beneficial for reconnecting with yourself.

Start to set boundaries with friends and family. Start setting up smaller boundaries with people in your life. Practice saying out loud what you want and don't allow anyone to step on your boundary. They may not like the new boundaries; you may even lose people along the way. That's okay! The more you enforce your boundaries, the more respect people will have for you. Additionally, you'll gain respect for yourself. The great thing about boundaries is that you decide what they are and if you need to change them, you can. I recommend thinking of each relationship you have that's causing discomfort, and see how you can change the dynamics. Maybe it's time to start saying no, allowing the other person to figure things out without your help.

Start looking at things you do.

Are they helpful or hurtful? Does it inspire and motivate? How do you talk to yourself in your own head? Do you feel that you're capable; do you trust yourself? This part is also really important if you want to make real change. There are so many of us who talk badly about ourselves in our own heads. How could we ever expect to find someone to love us in a healthy way if we don't even love ourselves in a healthy way?

Stop lying to yourself.

Most of us saw the red flags early in the relationships, but we ignored them. We may have ignored them because of our upbringing, the fairy tale stories we hear, we felt like we were already in too deep, or we simply didn't care! No matter what the reason is, it's important to be honest with yourself, and forgive! Denying what really happened in the relationship and how it affected you is not helpful for your healing. It's time to be honest.

Face whatever issues you need to from your childhood.

Wherever you felt lack, ignored, unimportant, or unattractive; instead of shying away from it, let yourself go there. If it's hard to come up with anything, start writing letters to family members or to your younger self. They don't have to be sent, but write it as if it will be. Just free write everything that comes to mind. After awhile you'll start to get to the root of whatever hurt exists. In some instances, you can have a face to face conversation with the person who hurt you and tell them what you were feeling. In other cases, you may have to settle for writing a letter and burning it - or choosing some kind of ritual to let the words and experience go. There are many great techniques you can use, but I've found this one to be helpful in getting my mind around different issues. Listen to how you talk

Stephanie McPhail

to the child inside, would you talk to a friend or your own child that way? No? Then take a lesson from that and change your inner child dialogue.

Learn how to take care of yourself.

It's really important to focus all of your attention on yourself during the healing process. If you have kids, make sure you're getting them help as well; you don't want the cycle to continue with them! If you've been neglecting your health, then get back on track with a healthy exercise and eating routine. Start meditation, yoga, reconnect with community and a higher power. It doesn't have to be religion but feeling connected to the world around you helps tremendously in healing.

Do not jump into another relationship!

I want so badly to put extra explantation points here! So many people jump right from one to another, continuing the same patterns in the next relationship. You got yourself out, don't start the same way all over again! I know it feels good to have someone attracted to you after you've felt unattractive and even unlovable for so long. However, it's more important for you to love yourself! Let yourself feel lonely! A new relationship right after an old one tends to happen because of avoidance and discomfort of looking within. Cry about it, it's okay! Allow yourself to feel the pain. You can't grow if everytime it hurts, you do something to cover up that feeling. New relationships will only get in the way of your focus, and your focus should be on yourself and discovering who's been hiding inside. Step into the pain, not away from it, by being by yourself for a while. This is where I got stuck so many times. i was always so focused on taking care of others and not being alone (that word used to be so scary!) that I was not able to focus on the issues that I needed to deal with! Everytime I would feel the pain I would do everything in my power to avoid really feeling it which lead me to recreate the same patterns over and over, which intellectually was the opposite of what I wanted to do! Going through my depression actually forced me to be alone, feel the pain and learn from it. Once you work on the areas you need to improve in then you will not attract the same type of people into your life. The amount of time will be different for everyone but I recommend starting with a year and then re-evaluating how you are feeling and go from there. Keep working on yourself and as your self-esteem and boundaries improves so will who you attract!

Spend time with people who are already in healthy relationships.

Don't sit with other unhappy people and commiserate on how bad he or she is/was. This will only cloud your brain with the thought that you have to settle. You'll question whether or not it's even possible for people to be happy in a relationship. You'll notice that hanging out with happy couples also helps you feel less stressed! Observe how they are together. See what's working for them. Observe how they speak to each other, even when they're irritated with each other. This will give you a better idea of what real love should feel like. Pay attention to how you feel around them.

The stories of romantic love in movies and books so often portray love as something you have to fight for. Love is something lost and then found. None of that is calm. If it makes you anxious, nervous, and keeps you from enjoying your own life - it's not healthy. None of that is real, long lasting love.

You may notice that after awhile, you really don't want to spend time with people who aren't happy in general because it may feel draining. Once you start the process of letting go of anyone who brings you down, you'll see that your tolerance for drama and comfort drops. You may not even notice as it happens because it might be subtle, or it may happen from one day to the next, but it will happen.

Learn to say no without worry that someone's going to be upset with you or that you feel you need to explain your reason.

This is not easy to do at first, but setting healthy boundaries gets easier with time. In the past, you may have said no but then felt really guilty about it and changed your mind. This time around, say no and even if it feels uncomfortable, stick to what you said.

People who think they can figure out how to change on their own have missed something very important. If it was so easy, you would've done it already! We seem to be afraid to rely on anyone, but sometimes you need to hire the right person for the job! If you've spent your whole life in codependent relationships, you may not be the best person to be in charge of your emotions and future relationships; your friends might not be either! Having someone who can tell you when they see red flags, and help you work through moments that at the time may be painful, is super important.

Do only what feels good.

I read a meme the other day "Treat yourself so well that when someone treats you badly you recognize it!" If it feels good, do it! If it feels bad, don't do it! It's pretty simple, but a lot of us haven't followed that rule. We did what we thought was best for someone else without thinking of ourselves and our feelings. Once you start to only follow what feels good, you won't be able to be with ANYONE who tries to take that away. Life is way more fun when you're spending time doing things you enjoy! Of course having the right support during this time is crucial so you don't start doing what "feels good" only because it's what you have been used to. You will notice the difference between discomfort because it is out of your comfort zone and discomfort because you know it's wrong for you. Look at the feelings in your body and pay close attention to the signals you are getting. It will get easier with practice.

Do things differently than you had before.

If something feels automatic for you, do something different. Some habits may be good and some may be bad. Look closely at some of the activities you do on a regular basis, and figure out if they're hurtful or helpful. If they don't add to you and your growth in any way, stop doing it.

Take action on creating the life you want to be living.

At the end of the day, you aren't living for me, your spouse, your family, or anyone else - you're living your own life! It's up to you to make changes if you don't feel like it's the life you want to be living. The great thing about being the author of your own story is you get to change the story whenever you want. To make changes, you're going to have to face discomfort to get to your goal. Change is not always comfortable, but it's worth it. Take control of your future, and start taking daily action steps that will move you forward. Continuing to think and act the way you always have will just keep you stuck in the same pattern. This is another part I really recommend a coach or a therapist for in order to hold you accountable on a weekly basis!

Be kind to yourself throughout your process!

It's a long process. There will be days you move forward, days you move backwards, and days you don't move at all! You are human. Don't let the ups and downs take over so you feel you can't do it. Keep reminding yourself how far you've come, look back at all the of the good things you've achieved, and let that remind you of your power to keep moving forward.

Chapter 8
Red Flags, Green Lights

"Remembering you are going to die is the best way I know to avoid the trap of thinking you have something to lose. You are already naked. There is no reason not to follow your heart." **Steve Jobs**

Okay. You got out, worked on yourself and now you're ready to start thinking about starting a new relationship. You don't want to fall into the same automatic patterns. What are red flags and green lights when starting new relationships?

I've done the bad relationships more than a few times. Now that I've finally figured out how to attract a positive, healthy relationship, I have a few tips based on life experience and books I've read about this topic. There were similarities in all of the toxic relationships. I've spoken to many people who have been in similar situations and their red flags seem to match up with mine.

Name calling!

I had actually almost forgotten to put this in the book because it has become so obvious to me now that I am in a healthier place. Every relationships that I had been in from my teen years until my mid 30's always included my partner losing their temper and calling me a "Bitch", "Whore" and even "Cunt." If you are in a relationships where there is any name calling at all, this is a huge red flag! It is never okay to disrespect your partner by calling them names meant to demoralize or degrade them. That is an issue with wanting power and control over another person. My husband David and I may get irritated at each other at times but we have never, nor will we ever, cross the line into name calling. It's normal to disagree sometimes. In fact, if different ideas are met with a healthy discussion, it can actually improve the bond and the relationship. However, the line should never be crossed into cursing and putting each other down. You need to keep in mind that if you love your partner, this disagreement will end. You don't want the words you say in anger to affect your relationship negatively in the future. Emotional abuse can hurt just as much as physical abuse. You must keep in mind that you are meant to support each other, not cut the other one down.

Wanting to go too fast!

Relationships take time to grow and nourish as you get to know someone for who they are. If someone's trying to tell you on the fourth date they love you and can imagine spending the rest of their lives with you, be extremely careful. This can be a red flag. If they're coming on too strong, too fast, it may be because they know that once you see who they really are, you won't be interested in them anymore. They want to suck you in before you "get away." The idea is, once you have feelings for them, they can relax and show you who they really are. For caretakers who haven't learned healthy boundaries (AKA people with codependency issues), this triggers a "let's help them" mode. If they're trying to rush you, and there's any feeling of discomfort, don't be afraid to speak up. If they agree to slow down, but then don't follow through, you know they aren't trustworthy. If they try to make you feel bad for giving them that boundary, you know it's time to go. No matter what they say, stick to your gut. If it feels off then it probably is.

How do they speak about exes and their family?

Do they still seem like a wounded animal who is licking their wounds and trying their best to move on? Do they talk a lot about how horrible their exes were and how angry they still are with them? Do they do the opposite and not talk about exes or family at all? What are they hiding? If they're showing a lot of emotion, they may not be over their ex. They're so wounded, they need to be told they're right. People like this still need to do a lot of work on themselves before they're ready to start dating again.

Do they shower you with money or gifts, and can their job support it?

Let's be honest, when we find someone who we enjoy spending time with, we start living in the now and looking forward to the next fun thing we're going to do with them. However, watch out for the red flag of using money and gifts as leverage. You may hear things like, "I spent so much money on that for you; I deserve this." It can easily be used to manipulate you. If they're keeping score of how many things they bought you, this is an early warning sign. Gifts shouldn't be given with expectations. As soon as that happens, it comes from the wrong place.

Even if gifts come with no strings attached, do they have the money to afford it? You have to ask yourself if you want to be with someone who doesn't care about money at all? Are you ready to support them and have large financial debt because their tastes are higher class than their budget allows? It's sweet and romantic when you start out, but it's a false start. You get used to that lifestyle, but it isn't realistic. You end up resenting each other; money and different spending styles can cause major rifts in relationships.

How are they with money in general?

Even in the happiest relationships, money can be the biggest reason why they end. Are you on the same page with spending practices? Are you both open and honest about how and where you spend your money? Have you gotten advice on how to properly balance your budget, and do you both follow it? Do you spend more than you make? If you're not sure how to make the most with what you have, don't be afraid to speak to a financial advisor. Avoiding this important topic will lead to much larger problems.

What are their friends and family like?

When you meet their family, are they welcoming of you? Do they start telling you to watch out for their brother/sister/child right away? Do you notice that one of their parents is a little too much in their business? Are friends constantly talking about your new partner's many mistakes? Do they ignore you when friends or family are around? These are all things to be wary of.

Do they ask you how your day was and actually seem interested in your answer?

Do they even bother to ask about your day? Do you feel like telling them? When you don't feel like you're being listened to, it's hard to share what's on your mind. If they ask about you, but seem to only care about what they're going to say for their response, they don't have good communication skills. A relationship is all about communication. The person you date and marry should be your best friend. You should be able to tell them anything and feel like you're understood. If you're not comfortable telling your partner whatever is on your mind and sharing mundane day to day stressors, then it's time to move on.

How do they react when you share your hopes and dreams?

This is related to the above answer, but there's more involvement with this answer. Yes, of course you need to be good communicators, but you also need to be a good support system for each other. If your partner immediately shuts down every dream or goal you have in life, they aren't for you. If they try to sabotage your path to your goals, they are not the right match. Partners should support each other in their passions and dreams. When my current husband David and I made our marriage vows, we included that we'd be supportive of each other's dreams. Here is a piece of the vows I wrote for him: *"I will always be on your side, your biggest cheerleader, reminding you not to lose sight of your goals and dreams. I'll be the kind of partner that helps us both stay inspired to be the best we can be."* His words to me were similar, and we didn't even know what either of us would write! Part of healthy love is to support each other's dreams.

How do they behave in stressful situations?

When things don't go right, what's their first reaction? Do they lose their temper? Do they overreact? Do they help ease your tension, or do they make you feel more stressed out? Think about the big things that can go wrong in life. Would you want to go through the worst times in life with them as your partner? You can

Stephanie McPhail

see who someone is when they start yelling at the person on the phone for not delivering the right object, instead of calmly asking to speak to a supervisor. That's little stuff compared to what you'd have to deal with if you were in a long term relationship with them.

How do they argue/fight?

Even if you've never had an argument with them yet, watch how they handle disagreements with friends or family. Do they default to yelling, cursing, blaming, and bringing up old stuff? Or do they stick to the problem at hand, and keep it to feelings and talking about how something has affected them? How they fight with others will be how they fight with you; don't think you're different.

Do they seem pushy or controlling?

If you tell them you're going out with friends, do they constantly call or text you or do they allow you to enjoy your time out? Do they tell you what to wear or who to hang out with? A healthy relationship allows for each person to have time away without feeling guilty or worried.

When you come back from being out, do they try and look through your phone or e-mails?

Are you afraid to leave your phone out because they'll go through it? Not that you have anything to hide, but even a silly message among friends will be misinterpreted by someone looking to be jealous! If you feel like you need to go through their phone or they go through yours, then talk to them. This is normally a sign of something wrong and the relationship most often needs to be ended.

Can you trust them?

Trust is a cornerstone of a relationship; without it, the relationship isn't healthy. If neither of you trust one another, that will create drama. Lots of drama in a relationship is draining on your mental health. No trust is a good sign to leave.

Insecurity and fear.

Does your partner constantly act insecure? Do they use fear to try to control or manipulate you? We all have insecurities, but they shouldn't be used against us. Insecurity and fear leads to control issues which leads to unhealthy relationships. Be careful of this red flag because sometimes it can be subtle.

Do they threaten to commit suicide if you leave?

Don't fall into this trap, but don't ignore it either. As a crisis counselor, I urge you to call the police to tell them this person is suicidal. This will do two things. It'll make them see they can't pull that card with you again, and it'll also keep them safe when they may not be thinking clearly. The last thing you want is to feel even slightly responsible for someone taking their own life, especially if you knew and did nothing. Take every mention of it seriously. If they have a plan in mind, it's important to share that with the police. If they have a gun it's even more important because they may change their mind and decide to hurt someone else. Don't be afraid to protect yourself, and don't let them try to manipulate you into feeling bad for them.

How are they with sex?

A healthy sex life is important in an adult romantic relationship; without it you're just friends! It's also important to be able to communicate and feel heard about your wants, desires, fantasy, likes, and dislikes. If they keep pushing for something you don't feel comfortable with, then this can be a red flag. It's a good idea to talk about sexual expectations in the beginning of a relationship which includes how often, pregnancy/children, other sexual partners, any sexually transmitted disease, types of sexual practices they want to engage in, and anything else that comes to mind. There are too many people who feel uncomfortable having these conversations and end up steering away from them. As a result, the proper intimacy for a sexual relationship isn't established, and expectations aren't shared, which can cause a rift in the relationship.

For some people, sex is the only thing that's keeping them in the relationship. Sex is only one part. Don't stay just because the sex is great; there's a whole lot more going on outside the bedroom. Real intimacy is a combination of a healthy sex life and a close best friend relationship.

Infidelity.

If you met each other because either of you weren't faithful to a spouse, then you've seen firsthand how they deal with unhappiness in a marriage, and it's not honestly. Don't fall into the trap of thinking that you're different and they won't do the same to you.

The important thing is to remove yourself from drama. If they keep accusing you, it could be a trust issue that they have from another relationship. How do both of you react to these feelings/accusations? If it is with care and honest communication then it may be helpful, but if there are more lies then trust will only further be broken. Living with a partner that doesn't trust you and vice versa makes for a very unhappy household for everyone.

Road rage?

How are they when they're driving? Do they tell stories of when they lost their temper while driving and got into a physical altercation with someone? Have they ever put you in danger with you or your child in the car? Road rage can be deadly and should be a huge red flag. If they can't control their temper on the road, how are they going to control their temper in other stressful situations? This also shows their true colors. Don't put your life, or anyone else's, in danger; an automobile is a deadly weapon!

If it feels forced - walk away.

Do you feel like you're trying too hard to make something work? Then it's probably not a good fit. There are a lot of wonderful people out there who aren't a good fit for us. If your relationship looks good on paper but doesn't work naturally in real life, then it's not right. Ask yourself if you're putting your wants and needs on the back burner because you want the relationship to work so badly. It's only going to get worse as time goes on. There should be a natural flow where both people feel at ease to be themselves.

Behavior vs. words.

Pay close attention to how they act instead of what they say they're going to do. There are many people who say one thing, but do something else. Don't fall in love with the idea of who they are, or the hopes of who they can be. Make sure you fall in love with who they actually are right now.

Chapter 9
Is everything perfect?

"I am not someone who is ashamed of my past. I'm actually really proud. I know I made a lot of mistakes, but they, in turn, were my life lessons."
Drew Barrymore

I cannot gush enough at how much happiness I feel in my heart. I remember too many times feeling like what I feel now could only be a dream. However, as someone who is in recovery from codependent/toxic relationships, I'm aware that I have to be more careful of my own behavior in this new relationship. I'm sharing some of these behaviors with you in the hopes it will help you take notice of some areas you may need to focus on as you move forward.

I am not perfect! I know this is a shock to everyone reading this (insert sarcasm here). This is important to remind ourselves. Whatever bad relationships you've had in the past aren't a reflection of you as a person. We can all learn from mistakes we have made! In hindsight, I could have ended it when I saw the first red flags, stopped pushing so much to make it work, been more open with friends/family about what was going on, been more honest with myself and my partner etc. I didn't then, but I can decide to not do that again. We are human and make mistakes; forgive yourself! These are things to recognize in my current healthy relationship so I don't fall into the same patterns again. I'll never again allow myself to get into a situation where I get to that level of negative.

Silence and not saying something on my mind when it happens. Avoiding conflict and avoiding resolutions: Sometimes, it's easier to overlook a few differences rather than pick a fight over it. If something bothers you, don't avoid talking about it with the person who's hurting you. It's really important to look at how you communicate and speak with a professional, after unhealthy relationships we can have unhealthy patterns. I realize there are still times when something happens and my automatic response is to have no response. I get irritated at things and I allow them to build up. I'm not saying you should say every little irritation that comes up, but maybe for a while you should! As you figure things out and learn what's important, you'll start to see the difference. Now when I feel frustrated with my husband, I look at what the problem is, think about why I'm feeling that way, and then explain the frustration or hurt and explain how it's affecting me even if saying it makes me feel uncomfortable. This keeps communication open and allows the discussion to be about solutions rather than each person defending their actions.

Being totally honest. Make sure you're honest with yourself about control and trying to fix your partner. Be honest about how you relate to others and yourself. Tell your partner anything and everything that's on your mind. Don't hold back your fears or frustrations. There shouldn't be any secrets from each other. This will help intimacy grow and help ensure you don't revert back to stuffing emotions, not dealing with them, and focusing on the other person's faults. You need to recognize your codependent behaviors so that you can choose more functional and healthier ones.

Learning when to walk away from an argument and giving space. I've realized that I'm someone who likes to get to the bottom of issues right away and not dwell on them, my husband need time to think things through. That's OK! Through lots of communication, we've come to realize that when there's an issue, we discuss it and then walk away. I'm more of an extrovert and he's more of an introvert; we deal with things differently. He needs time alone to process his feelings, which I have to allow him! In the past I kept pushing and feeling annoyed that he couldn't verbalize what he was feeling, but we realized he can't put it into words right away. Once we understood that, it made things much easier for both of us!

Take breaks from each other! My husband is my best friend and he's my favorite person in the world, next to my son, to hang out with. That doesn't mean we need to do everything together, as much as I want to! It took me so long to find a good partner, now I feel like I don't want to lose any more time! However, it's important to take time apart. Before you got together, you were able to live your own lives, and it's important to still have your own sense of self away from the relationship. I actually enjoy taking my son to the park by myself, or meeting up with a friend for some girl time. It's also nice to come back with new stories and experiences to share; it's hard to do that when you always do everything together!

Stop every once in awhile and ask yourself how you feel and what you want. As someone who has so often put my own needs to the side, this part has been super important. I go into automatic caretaking mode. It's a good idea to make sure you aren't keeping the people in your life from figuring things out on their own without constantly pointing things out. This is exhausting and doesn't allow room for the other person to grow. Re-centering helps remind me to keep my practice of self care and healthy boundaries in the forefront. I still do this pretty often because old habits can be hard to break. When we can recognize an issue, we can bring it into our own view so we can work on it. If not, it's easy to get back into the suppressing and codependent behavior of doing a lot of things for others at our own expense.

Be careful of staying in a place where you are a victim. This leads to a victim mentality. Even in writing this book, I did my best to tell the story without blaming. The person who hurt you probably would've hurt anyone they were in an intimate partnership with. It just happened to be you because you weren't equipped with the knowledge yet to empower yourself to get away. Keep using empowering words when speaking about yourself. You truly have control over how your life will end up, depending on what lessons you learn along the way. Listen to them so you don't repeat them.

Desires and expectations. Do you have secret expectations about your partner, something you haven't told them but expect them to do or know? Or do you have aspirations you wish your partner could help you achieve? It's important for my husband and I to communicate openly and honestly everything that's on our mind. A lot of times if there's an issue with us, it's because we didn't adequately communicate what our expectation was to the other person. Lay it all on the line and when new things come up, add them to the list.

Dominance and control. A healthy relationship should have an equal balance of power between the partners. There may be times where that slightly changes and shifts, but it should go back to equal afterwards. My husband and I are very different people and have different work patterns. We came into the relationship as two whole people looking to share in life's journey together, not "two halves looking to completed each other." This is important to keep in mind. Different people act differently. Sometimes I get frustrated when I don't feel like he's doing "enough." I've realized that when I come from a place where I'm feeling a need to control him to do what I want, I take a step back. I have to remind myself he has his own journey and I can really only control myself. Seeing it instead as a sign of working on patience helps me stay focused on the real issue: why am I looking to control what he's doing? I married him as an adult, whole man who's been able to take care of himself for a long time. It's not fair for me to suddenly take away his own strength in making decisions for himself; it's disempowering. If you feel like you are being dominated or not given enough control of the relationship and its direction, speak about it with your partner.

Now that you have more information and tools to start creating the life you want get out there and start taking action steps! The more quickly you start the more fresh the information is! Stop waiting for things to change and start creating the change you are looking for! This is your life, and if it is the only one we get it's up to you to make it the best one possible! Get the right team to support you on your journey and start living your best life yet! Sending love and strength to all of you beautiful souls and never forget, you aren't alone in this journey but change really is up to you!

"Being Loved Shouldn't Hurt"

Quick Step Guides

181

Rediscovering Yourself after an Unhealthy Relationship
My Quick 7 Step Guide

After spending 15+ years of my life in unhealthy, abusive relationships, I finally took some important steps to take back control of my life and happiness. I was then able to find and marry the man of my dreams. I'm thankful for the lessons I learned along the way and would like to share some of these tips with you; I promise it's worth the work!

Seven steps to rediscover yourself are as follows:

1. **Get out of your "Comfort Zone."** Try things that make you uncomfortable. I used to be afraid of heights. I have now jumped out of an airplane three times and even took a flying lesson! Once I did that, I realized how much I enjoyed it and understood that I may have missed out on so much more because of my fear! You can open up a whole new world for yourself just by trying new things.

2. **Learn what love feels like.** When I was in unhealthy relationships, I thought love was uncomfortable and stressful. Being around people who help you stay calm is a good start. When certain people start to make you feel anxious or uncomfortable, get away from them. Feeling the need to be "polite" can keep us in bad situations.

Once you learn the calmness of love, you won't go back to what was unhealthy because you won't put up with it.

3. **Know thyself.** Get to know who you are without another relationship. Chances are good you've been trying to make everyone else happy for so long, you don't even know how to make yourself happy anymore. Learn what makes you tick. What do you enjoy? Dislike? What are your little idiosyncrasies? What do you feel you need to work on for yourself? You need to do this for you, not for anyone else.

4. **Find a hobby.** In fact, find several! Try anything that seems even slightly interesting to you! Give it a few tries to see if it's a good fit. It'll get you out meeting new people and it'll also help you find healthier ways to deal with life's ups and downs. Additionally, you'll become stronger and more resilient! You'll feel better; therefore, you won't want to be around people who don't add to that feeling! Yoga and meditation are pretty amazing if you're looking for somewhere to start.

5. **Travel.** Make a list of all the places you'd like to see. Figure out how to get there. Life is short and there are many beautiful places! Don't have the money? Start saving. Think that'll take too long? There are some wonderful apps available that can help you travel for a very low cost. I used couchsurfing.com to get free room and board

across the country! Where there is a will, there's a way. Don't have anyone to go with? Go by yourself, and if you have kids, bring them along. I traveled by myself and LOVED the freedom to do whatever my heart desired. I met some pretty cool people along the way, too!

6. **Start a healthy eating and exercise routine.** It's easy to get into a slump when you aren't feeling happy, but this can become a vicious cycle. Eating well and exercising will give you more energy and help with your confidence, while also improving your overall health. Who doesn't want to live a longer and healthier life when they're creating so much joy and excitement!?!

7. **Date!** Once you've gotten comfortable with all of these other steps, start dating. Sign up for the dreaded online dating sites. Get out of the house and into situations where you can meet new people. Be true to yourself; someone amazing is out there searching for someone like you. Make first dates short and in public places. After each encounter, add to your list of wants and don't wants that we talked about earlier.

7 Early Warning Signs of an Unhealthy Relationship

1. **They want to spend all of your free time together.** This sounds sweet, but if you're spending all of your time together, what are they neglecting? Do they have friends and hobbies that are also important to them? If they don't, they need to keep working on themselves and probably aren't ready for a committed relationship yet. It may also be a sign of jealousy: they're afraid you'll find someone else.

2. **Excessive calls/texts.** It's nice to receive messages from a new love interest. However, if you're out with friends and constantly have to look at your phone to make sure you aren't missing a message because they'll get upset with you, that's a red flag! This is a sign they're jealous and want you all to themselves.

3. **Love Bombing/moving too quickly.** If someone starts planning a future with you and asking you to move in on the second date, run! These are signs they're worried they're going to lose you and want to "snag you in." If they can get you to see a future together, it's way easier to look past other issues you may be noticing. It takes time to really fall in love with

someone. Becoming best friends in addition to having a sexual relationship is an important aspect of healthy relationships.

4. **Being intimidated by you.** Does the person you're with say they're intimidated by you? This normally means they'll try to bring you down; it's a huge red flag.

5. **How do they speak to you? Do they appreciate all areas of you?** I was often told that I spoke too loud or tried too hard to be the center of attention. If anyone tries to dull your shine, move along. There's someone out there looking for all the great qualities you have; don't let yourself down by settling for someone who doesn't support who you are.

6. **How do they behave when they're frustrated?** How are they when they don't get what they want? How are they when someone makes them angry on the road? Watch these interactions closely. It's easier to notice when it's happening directly to you, but be careful of how they are with other people. If they're capable of losing their temper with others, they're equally able to lose it with you.

7. **How do they disagree?** Are you both able to have a disagreement without name calling, physical violence, or yelling? The moment names are called, respect is gone. If you allow this to happen by staying, it'll snowball from

"Being Loved Shouldn't Hurt"

here. This is never OK in a healthy relationship. Stick to the problem and the feelings at hand and listen to each other.

6 Ways to Keep Your Energy Levels Up

1. **Plant-based diet.** This keeps me from feeling weighed down and sluggish from my food; instead, it energizes me.
2. **Green smoothies and hydration.** Green Smoothies keep my nutrients high and water keeps me well hydrated. Most people are tired because they're lacking these two criteria.
3. **Exercise, yoga, meditation, and get outdoors.** These have been a part of my regular routine for a while now. They all increase my energy, help me to refocus, and ground me.
4. **No TV!** Sitting on the couch is one of the quickest ways for me to lose motivation. As soon as the television goes on, I get sucked in and pay attention to nothing else. It's also filled with negativity and unhealthy habits. Not viewing these things helps me stay in the now and appreciate what I have in front of me.
5. **Stay away from "drama."** If I feel anyone or anything trying to drain my energy, I remove myself from it. If I have no choice but to be around it anyway, I counteract it as quickly as possible with coping mechanisms from number 3.

6. Do what feels good. If I feel a "pull" to do something, I follow that gut reaction. The things that come natural are an easy way to keep my energy up. I really listen to my body for this one; if I feel a positive feeling in my stomach or chest I do it, if I don't feel that, I stay away from it. This makes it easy to make important decisions.

9 Tips On How To Get Out Safely

I recommend you contact your local Domestic Violence organization to find out what's available to you in your community and what local laws are. Please keep your safety in mind since this is the most dangerous time for you and your children. Here are some of the things I did:

1. **Save up money, as much as you can.** I'd take $100 at a time and hide it in the back of my stocking drawer in case I had to grab money and run. When things got worse, I kept a bag of clothes, money, and important paperwork in a bag in my car. You may not have the ability to do this, but if you can, it's a good idea.

2. **You need to be the one who leaves.** This gives you power back over your life. It's so important to make the first move. If you leave a shared residence, be prepared to never see any of your stuff again. If you have pets, I understand they may try to use their safety against you. Do everything in your power to bring them with you but if you can't, you need to think of your safety (and if you have kids, their safety) as a priority. Even if your relationship doesn't have as much violence, it's still best for you to leave first. Just removing yourself from whatever chaos is going on at home is better for your sanity.

3. **Find a place to stay.** It's best to be somewhere they can't find you or put you and your family in danger. If you have to go to a shelter, then go. It's temporary; this period will pass. If you don't leave then you'll keep living the nightmare forever.

4. **If you have even the slightest feeling that you could be in danger: Go to the police, press charges, and file a restraining order.** Most police stations have a domestic violence advocate or there are local agencies that will go with you to properly fill out the forms. Don't feel bad about using local agencies. They're free and they're there for you.

5. **Call your phone company and make sure you have a password associated with your account.** If you can't block them for whatever reason, then change your number. If you have children and you need to keep in contact with your ex, then decide with your lawyer, in writing, what that communication will look like.

6. **Go grey rock.** They're going to try to do whatever they can to get you back. They'll sweet talk and say all of the right things. It's important to remind yourself you've been down this road before. They'll never change. After you don't respond to the sweet messages, the nasty ones might start. Don't read the messages or listen to

the voicemails, but don't delete them. It's important to save them.

7. **If you're married, especially if you have kids, then get a lawyer right away.** Chances are pretty good they won't play nice because they want to get back at you for ending the cycle. I know they can be expensive, and that's an issue for many people. Your safety is priceless.

8. **Be prepared for gaslighting**. This is the term used to describe what happens so often at the end of the relationship. It means that the other person is making up information to try to make themselves look or feel better about the breakup. Allow them to say whatever they want to say. The right people will know right away what's really going on. Other people will see the truth in time.

Codependency/Toxic Relationship Checklist

Here's a list of typical characteristics of someone who is codependent. Take out a piece of paper and make a checklist, or check them off right in your book if it's related to you. If you notice that you're checking off a lot of these statements, it's extra important to get someone to help you make changes! They include but aren't limited to:

- Do you always need things to be perfect and fear failure?
- Do you feel guilty setting boundaries?
- Do you feel like a victim?
- Are you sensitive to criticism?
- Do you focus on other people's wants instead of your own needs?
- Are you uncomfortable receiving attention?
- Do you feel responsible for the feelings or actions of others?
- Do you have low self esteem or a weak sense of identity?
- Do you feel alone, abandoned, angry, sad, ashamed, or helpless?
- Do you blame others for how you feel, and wait for someone to come save you?
- Do you feel empty, bored, and worthless unless you have someone to take care of or a crisis to solve?

- Do you do everything your new partner does, forgetting about your own interests? Do you find it difficult to find satisfaction in other aspects of your life?
- Do you see toxic behavior from your partner but find it difficult to admit you're in a dysfunctional relationship?
- Do you stay in unhealthy relationships, not vocalizing your needs and tolerating abuse in order to keep people loving you?
- Do you go from one bad relationship to another one?

About The Author

Stephanie received her BS in Psychology from SUNY New Paltz and her double Master's in Education and Health from Hofstra University. Her experience working as a specialist, trainer, and educator for a crisis intervention and suicide prevention hotline led to her passion for educating people on how to live their most fulfilling lives.

Her pursuit of continuing education led to additional certifications in nutrition, various teaching modalities, and working with special needs children; all of which contributed to a well-rounded perspective on wellness. Possessing an innate awareness of our energetic nature, Stephanie was led to become certified as a level 2 Reiki practitioner. Recognizing a greater calling to inspire others to achieve results reflective of their true potential, she became a Transformational Coach and was certified as a Dream Coach®. She enables her clients to gain clarity on their true purpose and create a workable action plan to make their greatest dreams a reality.

Stephanie lives in New York with her husband David and children where she takes coaching clients and runs an online holistic healing center alongside her husband.

Stephanie McPhail

References

"Co-Dependency." Mental Health America, Mental Health America, www.mentalhealthamerica.net/co-dependency.

Beattie, Melody. Codependent No More. MJF Books, 1992.

Hammond, Christine. "The Narcissistic Cycle of Abuse." The Exhausted Woman, PsychCentral, 4 May 2017, pro.psychcentral.com/exhausted-woman/2015/05/the-narcissistic-cycle-of-abuse/.

Hammond, Christine. "Loneliness: A Constant Battle Seen with Personality Disorders." PsychCentral, PsychCentral, 22 Sept.2017, pro.psychcentral.com/exhausted-woman/2017/09/loneliness-a-constant-battle-seen-with-personality-disorders/.

"Patterns and Characteristics of Codependence." Co-Dependents Anonymous International, Co-Dependents Anonymous, Inc., 2011, coda.org/index.cfm/meeting-materials1/patterns-and-characteristics-2011/.

Made in the USA
Middletown, DE
15 June 2019